Find Us
Faithful

David Olford

Find Us Faithful

Leadership that Leaves a Legacy

B&H
PUBLISHING GROUP

NASHVILLE, TENNESSEE

ISBN: 978-0-8054-4548-0
B&H Publishing Group
Nashville, Tennessee
www.BHPublishingGroup.com

Dewey Decimal Classification: 303.3
Subject Heading: Leadership / Paul—Apostle / Bible N.T. Acts 20:17–35

Printed in the United States
1 2 3 4 5 6 7   12 11 10 09

To Dad

The Reverend Dr. Stephen F. Olford
(1918–2004)

Find Us Faithful

We're pilgrims on the journey
Of the narrow road
And those who've gone before us
Line the way
Cheering on the faithful
Encouraging the weary
Their lives a stirring testament
To God's sustaining grace

Oh, may all who come behind us
Find us faithful
May the fire of our devotion
Light their way
May the footprints that we leave
Lead them to believe
And the lives we live
Inspire them to obey
Oh, may all who come behind us
Find us faithful

Surrounded by so great
A cloud of witnesses
Let us run the race
Not only for the prize
But as those who've
Gone before us
Let us leave to those behind us
The heritage of faithfulness
Passed on through godly lives

After all our hopes and dreams
Have come and gone
And our children sift through all
We've left behind
May the clues that they discover
And the mem'ries they uncover
Become the light that leads them
To the road we each must find.*

Table of Contents

Preface

This book started behind my back! More accurately, it began without my knowledge. My father died at around 11:15 p.m. on Sunday night, August 29, 2004. Soon after his death, I received a letter dated August 30 from Anita Bosley. Mrs. Bosley had worked with us on a number of publishing projects, and this letter was to make me aware of one that my father had initiated without my knowledge. Here are some excerpts from her letter:

> Dear Dr. David,
>
> Several weeks ago, your father called me and asked if I could meet with him, as he had something very important to discuss with me. The excitement and urgency in his voice were apparent. Within a few hours, I was seated in his study listening as he outlined his vision.
>
> Your father wanted to give you a gift—something to encourage you in your ministry, something that would let you know how much he thought of what you have become in Christ. It was his great desire that you be published. It was his wish that, from a series of your lectures and sermons, I work to create for you the beginnings of a book—something with a substantial foundation from which you could expand, revise, and then publish.
>
> He selected the series himself. The series he chose was one you did on radio, "Three Legacies of a Faithful Ministry." Over the course of several weeks, I transcribed the tapes and edited the manuscript. I finished the project on the Monday he went in for surgery.

Looking back, I am awed with God's tremendous grace in providing your father with the vision and the vehicle by which to make this project a reality. It is my prayer that this manuscript will serve as a catalyst for you. This is a father's gift to his beloved son.

Serving Him,
Anita Bosley

I was not able to thank my father or to discuss this project with him due to his unexpected death. But I certainly have a sense of personal obligation and responsibility to fulfill his vision and complete it. I do so, though, not because something has been dumped on me as a burden. No. I have accepted his very special gift to me, and I want to use it as it should be used. Hence, the pages before you right now! But being the wise father and leader that he was, my father selected material that was and is vitally important to me. So the starting place for this book, textually and topically, is one that I have embraced wholeheartedly.

My father selected the "farewell address" of the apostle Paul in Acts 20 as the starting place for this book. I don't think I can adequately express the appropriateness of his selection. My father was not able to give us a farewell address because of his sudden stroke. As I remarked at his memorial service, he did not need to call us to his side for a bedside speech. He had left nothing unsaid, and in that sense we had nothing we needed to hear. He did not need to give us a "farewell address" as such.

It is deeply significant to me that the basic truths and thrust of the apostle Paul's amazing address in Acts 20 could have been expressed by my father himself if he had been able to say good-bye in Memphis, if not Miletus. I point out this connection between my father's death and Paul's departure for three reasons.

First of all, I want to honor my father, for he certainly was faithful to the end in life and ministry. When I think of faithfulness, my father immediately comes to mind.

Second, I want you to know what is actually behind the writing of this book, how this book started, and why it addresses particular issues. When dealing with issues of faithfulness, leadership, and ministry, there could be many legitimate starting places. This personal information helps to explain what is before you.

Last, I would like to think that one of the primary motivations for the writing of this book is directly related to the primary message of this book. This book deals with the subject of faithfulness—specifically the subject of faithfulness in ministry and leadership. My father's faithfulness started this book, and I needed to be faithful to complete the job. That was a personal motivation on my part. But this personal motivation is only part of the burden behind this book, for faithfulness is important and desperately needed in our day. If I am just another voice calling for biblical faithfulness, well, thank the Lord, the job has been worth the effort. We need to sound this message in a day when unfaithfulness is almost the norm or "just the way it is."

Responsibilities and busyness over the last few years are my excuses for not having written this book before now. I know all about being on a ministry treadmill and how hard it is to get off, or even change speeds. But I hope this delay is to your benefit. I may be more able to write this book now. Hopefully, the result will be a better book.

I am indebted to mention several major factors that contributed to the completion of this book. First of all, I want to thank B&H Publishing Group for taking on the project. I appreciate each person with B&H who has had a part in this along the way. Second, I appreciate greatly the sabbatical granted to me by Dr. David Dockery and Union University as I transitioned into a new role as the Stephen Olford Professor of Expository Preaching at Union University. This book was not my only project, but it was one that needed dedicated time, which the sabbatical provided. Sincere thanks is due also to the board of Olford Ministries International, Inc., who requested this sabbatical as we partnered with Union University, probably knowing that I would be a (more) serious "basket case" without it. I need to thank

Dr. Guy Richardson for the hospitality extended to me on my study visits to Reformed Theological Seminary (Jackson, Mississippi), and to Dr. Bryan Chapell for similar visits to the retreat facility at Covenant Theological Seminary (Kirkwood, Missouri). Special thanks is due to Anita Bosley, not only for her original work to start this project but also for her excellent editorial assistance as the new manuscript was produced. Many other friends and colleagues could be mentioned, but I just say "thank you" to all those who have had a part directly or indirectly in the publishing of this book.

Outside of the Lord Himself, who is worthy of all praise, glory, and honor, I must express my appreciation and thankfulness to my family:

To my mother, Mrs. Heather Olford, who continues to live faithfully "unto the Lord" after my father's death;

To my brother, Dr. Jonathan Olford, whose ministry and heart for those in crisis is exemplary;

To my daughters Lindsay and Stephanie, who are such a joy and blessing on a daily basis;

And especially to my wife, Ellen, who has been faithful not only to the Lord but also to me throughout our life together.

This book is written with the firm conviction that God Himself is faithful. That is ultimately why faithfulness matters, what faithfulness looks like, and how faithfulness is possible. Praise His Name!

Great is Thy faithfulness! Great is Thy faithfulness!
Morning by morning new mercies I see;
All I have needed, Thy hand hath provided;
Great is Thy faithfulness, Lord, unto me.[1]

Dr. David L. Olford
Memphis, Tennessee

Introduction

Few would question the need for faithful leaders and good leadership in our day. This need for good leadership crosses the various spheres of human relationships and activities in our world. And I would submit that the more chaotic our world seems to be and the more complex our world's problems, the more concerned people are about leadership. This does not negate cynicism, indifference, or frustration—all of which certainly abound as well—but most people who are concerned for societal or global problems are concerned about leadership issues.

As I write these words, we are in an election year in the United States. It is fascinating to watch all that is taking place during these pre-election months. Candidates, political parties, campaign strategies, major issues, potential scandals, speeches, debates, analyses, polls, commercials, mistakes, corrections, momentum, and much more dominate the media.

All of these pre-election processes and activities seem a long way from Moses and the burning bush, and they are! I do not say this to criticize what takes place today but simply because it's true! At the same time, there is something that ties together the human process of electing a president and God's initiative in calling Moses into a major leadership role. Both processes affirm the importance of getting the "right" person in leadership. Though the "burning bush" approach would seem more reliable, I do believe that somewhere in the midst of all of the hype and hoopla of an election is a concern on the part of many for a true leader. By a true leader, I mean someone who will be faithful to important principles and faithful to the people of the country. I know there are many other concerns and subplots, but despite the differing definitions or descriptions of what a faithful leader looks like, many people (in the end) still want such a person in charge.[1]

Many churches today are going through difficult times in terms of leadership and leadership issues. This is not a new thing, but it is a *real* thing. Dismissals, church conflicts, and church splits abound, and often leadership decisions and issues are at the center of it all. In a time of rapid change and with an influential culture impacting the church, leadership issues seem to intensify. Many models and expectations for leaders are available (with more or less biblical support). But despite all the confusion and evidences of the "flesh" in the church of Jesus Christ, there are those who still desire to have ministry leaders faithful to the Lord, His Word, and to the people they serve. What such faithful leadership looks like, especially in the church of Jesus Christ, is what this book is all about.

I simply want in the following pages to describe faithful leadership—faithful Christian leadership specifically—and encourage us to pursue such a standard for our own lives and the lives of other leaders. I hope to do this by presenting some biblical instruction, examples, and models that will challenge and encourage us to think about being faithful leaders within the sphere of influence God has given. And of course, I hope that such thinking will lead to more faithfulness in our personal character and the actual practice of leadership in the future.

I know this book is not unique in its burden nor in its appeal to the Scriptures for the truths and examples that will be set forth. It is my hope, though, that what is written will be truthful, meaningful, and helpful. At the same time, by going to various key Scripture passages, I desire to let the Scriptures do the talking as much as possible. Good things happen when we look to the Scriptures afresh with an open heart and mind in order to hear and obey what God would say to us.

Our Starting Place

We must begin by stating that leadership and faithfulness are eternally united in God Himself. God as Sovereign is "Leader" by definition. At the same time, from Genesis to Revelation, the faithfulness of God is revealed, proclaimed, and celebrated. God is the Faithful Leader, according to His eternal purposes and plans over creation, including mankind. This leadership is especially presented in terms of how God relates to His own people. A study of our great God and His dealings with His creation and His people would be instructive in and of itself. The same can be said of a thorough study of our Lord Jesus Christ. I leave these lifetime pursuits to you; both studies are beyond the parameters of this book. So let's start with just a few observations concerning some biblical data related to leadership.

Mankind was given leadership/stewardship responsibilities in God's first mandate to those who were created in His image (Gen. 1:26–28). Throughout the Scriptures, God consistently prepared, called, enabled, and used leaders for His special purposes. Moses, Joshua, Samuel, David, Solomon, and many others come to mind. Israel itself had a God-given leadership structure rather than being a loose-fitting group of autonomous individuals functioning independently from one another. Much teaching concerning good and bad leadership is presented in the historical books of the Old Testament alongside the explicit instructions found in the wisdom literature. Direct challenges to and correction of leadership are found in the prophetic books.

Our Lord Jesus was a leader with followers, even though He spoke of Himself as One who came to serve rather than to be served (Mark 10:45). He called a select group to Himself for training and preparation in order to initiate, humanly speaking, His mission to "make disciples" after His departure (Matt. 28:18–20). Thus, Jesus selected and trained men to become leaders, even though He defined leadership for His disciples in contrast to the Gentile world (Mark 10:42–44). In the early Christian mission, leaders were appointed to oversee local churches (Acts 14:23; 20:17–38). Other roles of responsibility are seen in Acts 6 and 15. Christ is viewed (by the apostle Paul) as the "Head" of the church, to whom He has given gifted individuals to lead and serve the church with the goals of ministry, unity, and maturity (Eph. 4:11–16; also Rom. 12:3–8; 1 Cor. 12–14). Qualifications for leaders are spelled out in a number of

New Testament epistles (1 Tim. 3:1–16; Titus 1:5–9; 1 Pet. 5:1–4). Paul's specific instructions to Timothy (especially) and to Titus give us a model for leadership and ministry training alongside the training of the twelve by our Lord. Numerous other texts of Scripture could be mentioned to indicate the importance of leadership in the church context, but we cite these just to remind us that leadership is of God and is part of God's will and plan for His people.

In Romans 13:1–7 the role of authority figures/ministers (and structures) for society is strongly affirmed, as is the Christian's responsibility to those who are in authority. This was a "live issue" in the AD fifties as followers of Christ sought to live in a world becoming more and more hostile to its claims and its very existence. In mentioning this one important biblical text, we have just started to scratch the surface of this aspect of the Christian's view of authority and leadership outside the church and in the world at large. Throughout the Scriptures, God is declared to be sovereign over the nations and leaders, but the legitimacy of leadership itself is affirmed under God's sovereign rule and purposes.

Defining Christian Leadership

Before we look at biblical texts to help us see what faithful Christian ministry and leadership are all about, I want to deal with some definitions. There are numerous definitions and descriptions of leadership. Ted Engstrom described leadership along these lines:

> The one characteristic common to all leaders is the ability to make things happen—to act in order to help others work in an environment within which each individual serving under him finds himself encouraged and stimulated to a point where he is helped to realize his fullest potential to contribute meaningfully....
>
> We might say, then, that leadership is an act or behavior required by a group to meet its goals, rather than a condition.

It is an act by either word or deed to influence behavior toward a desired end.[2]

The key word here is "influence," with the emphasis being on the leader's influence of others, with goals or "a desired end" in mind. Dr. Engstrom was concerned specifically with Christian leadership, but the preceding words could be used of leadership in general as well.

In terms of Christian leadership, J. Robert Clinton writes, "A leader is a person, 1) with God-given capacity and 2) with God-given responsibility who is influencing 3) a specific group of God's people 4) toward God's purposes for the group."[3]

Again, the concept of "influence" is central to the understanding of leadership, but it is worded here in terms of the context of the people of God specifically.

My concern, as I have said, is to address issues having to do with being a faithful Christian leader. *Christian leadership* (as a subset of leadership in general) *takes place when a Christian influences another or others through Christ and for Christ.* It is more formally Christian leadership when this influence is intentional, and it leads toward Christ-honoring goals. It is assumed, in the light of what we have said above, that this leadership is of God and is under the sovereign leading of God.

There are, I suppose, almost countless ways to assess and analyze Christian leadership. At the simplest level, there is the leader, the leading, and the one, the group, or the many who are being led. Focusing on the leader himself, such issues as calling, gifting, preparation, personal development, qualifications, responsibilities, styles, and the like can all receive attention. You can focus also on the leadership process. This involves all the dynamics of influence: motives, means, methods, movements, mechanics, measures, and various models of the processes involved when a person relates to others in a leadership role. You can focus, of course, on those being led and how the led actually respond to leadership, for those being led are also part of the leadership process as they are moved toward change, actions, goals, and so forth.

Where We Are Going

I mention these aspects of leadership to indicate that there is much ground to cover if one is seeking to be thorough in a study of leadership itself. That is not my intention. You need to read other books, such as the books listed in the bibliography, to get a better and bigger picture of broader leadership issues. As mentioned in the preface, the original starting place for this book was a study of Acts 20:17–38. The whole dynamic of this text makes it worthy of special attention in relation to the subject of faithful leadership. A leader is addressing other leaders at a critical time of closure and empowerment. A leader is speaking at a time that calls for priority issues to be addressed. Much can be gained by just reading and re-reading this passage of Scripture and meditating upon it.

But we don't end our study with Paul's words spoken to the elders from Ephesus. With the help of additional Scripture texts, I have sought to address other matters that relate to faithfulness in leadership. Rather than just talking about leadership matters and mentioning relevant biblical texts, I have sought to try to bring out of the selected texts truths, examples, implications, and applications that help us think about how to be faithful as Christian leaders. This is my approach in this book. Rather than presenting a systematic topical treatment of leadership issues, supplying easy bullet-point steps to follow, I have sought to let the Scriptures speak to us and challenge us on vital personal matters related to being faithful, especially as leaders. There are too many experiential variables to provide simple steps for everyone. But we can look toward the Scriptures to gain truths, insights, examples, and models that will help us examine our own lives and seek to move forward prayerfully, conscientiously, and by God's grace, courageously.

I have divided the studies ahead into three sections. The first section deals with "Legacies to Leave." Being faithful means living with the end in mind, preparing to give a "good account" by the grace of God. The next section seeks to cover "Responsibilities to Fulfill." Here we'll look at some key areas of life and ministry that need to be handled faithfully. Last, we'll consider some "Encouragements to Embrace." The road is long and difficult in the way of faithfulness, but there is much encouragement in the Lord and from the Word.

I write as one who seeks to be on this road, and as one facing the challenges involved. Many lessons have been learned from others and from personal experience (especially from mistakes). I am grateful for the many years of service alongside a faithful Christian leader, my father. His example has been a primary influence upon my life. I dedicate this book to my father (posthumously) in the light of the legacy of faithful Christian ministry and leadership that he left to us and in us.

Part One:
Legacies to Leave

CHAPTER 1
The Legacy of a Personal Example

There is an urgency about the matter of faithfulness. I am not just saying this to be dramatic or because I am now over fifty. Yes, I do realize that time is limited. More days are probably behind me than in front of me. But this isn't about my sense of finitude. Nor am I speaking about the condition of things in our world today, even though this is a cause for deep—and I mean deep—concern. Rather, there is a more basic issue related to this matter of faithfulness that confronts all of us. It is the giving of our attention to priority concerns and matters while we have the God-given time and opportunity to do so. We never know how much time we have in any given relationship, responsibility, ministry, or situation. And because of the awareness of the potential brevity of any season, we need to determine what really matters, what really counts, and what really must be done. We must be occupied faithfully with what God wants us to be and do in any given relationship or situation before we have to say, "Good-bye."

There is a sense in which faithfulness demands that we be ready to say a good "good-bye" at any moment. This may be said to friends, to associates, to a church, to a ministry, to a responsibility, to a season in life, or even to life itself. But it is wonderful if it can be said with the deep personal conviction that, by God's grace and according to His will, I was faithful to the Lord and to His will for me.

Take a few moments right now to do something. Imagine that God is calling you specifically and immediately to move away from where you are today in order to start a new phase of life, ministry, etc. Practically speaking, you will be disconnecting from the relationships and responsibilities that have been a major part of your life most recently. Let's say you were to meet with some close friends and share with them some parting words. What would you say? What would you cover in your "farewell address"? Go ahead. Write a few thoughts down. What would you like to say, especially about your own goals and activities that have been the "stuff" of your life?

The challenge before us in this chapter is to live each day in the light of our own "farewell address." When I speak of such an address, of course, I am not talking about some casual after-dinner speech, almost given without thinking. I am talking about the type of address that we hear all too rarely in our day. I'm talking about a solid statement and declaration of the God-given priorities and passions of our life. The address might remind those present of the key events and experiences you have shared together. Possibly you would share your personal goals and expectations for the future. Such an address might seek to exhort and empower those present to be faithful to the Lord themselves as they face the days ahead in your absence.

Talking about a farewell address may sound like the *last* chapter of a book rather than the first. But when you are thinking about faithfulness, you need to think backwards. Faithfulness has to do with the whole story, not just the beginning. It has to do with more than the start and more than the race. It especially has to do with the finish. Faithfulness is seen at the end of things and must be lived with the end of things in view. That is why I am encouraging you to live in light of your farewell address.

Acts 20:17–38 contains a God-given account of what can be viewed as a farewell address. To be accurate, when I use the phrase "farewell address," I am not presenting an argument for a specific rhetorical style in the technical sense.[1] I am using this phrase to describe what is, in fact, an account of the apostle Paul's parting words on a very significant occasion.

Paul here is at a critical point in his life and ministry. He is "hurrying to be at Jerusalem, if possible, on the Day of Pentecost" (Acts 20:16). He is finishing his third missionary journey and is heading to Jerusalem with funds collected for "the poor among the saints who are in Jerusalem" (Rom. 15:26). According to his letter to the Romans, Paul saw a season of ministry coming to a close and a new phase of ministry ahead (15:22–33). No doubt, the collection project had significance beyond the funds themselves, as it represented the fruit of the Gentile mission and the concern of the Gentile believers for their Jewish brethren in need. This was important to Paul.

The apostle chose not to travel to Ephesus where he had ministered extensively a few years earlier. At the same time, he obviously felt compelled to make contact with the church leaders in Ephesus and speak to them. So he sent for them. We are not told explicitly what was involved in getting word to Ephesus. We are also not given the details of how the leaders made their way to Paul some thirty miles away in Miletus.[2] Time and energy must have been expended for these elders to get there. But even though Luke does not give us many details about the arrangements for the meeting, he does give us details concerning what Paul said.

So here is the apostle, the one who had pioneered the mission in Ephesus and had founded the church there. He is entering a new phase of life and ministry, and only the Lord knows the details and detours of Paul's life that were to take place in coming years. The leaders, the elders of the church, come to see him at his request. Paul speaks to them. He speaks his mind and shares his heart. And in the middle of his address, he clearly reveals that these leaders will not see him again (Acts 20:25). As Luke concludes the narrative of this event, he paints a touching picture of prayer, tears, embraces, kisses, and sorrow. Then the group sees Paul to the ship to send him off. Luke's simple commentary is that at the heart of the sorrow was the fact that they were not going to see Paul again (v. 38).

Our focus is on what Paul said on this occasion and what we can learn from his words about faithfulness in ministry and leadership. The address itself is filled with reminders, examples, exhortations, warnings, goals, and personal remarks. Paul certainly defended his ministry record in Ephesus, explained his plans, and exhorted these leaders to be faithful in their appointed responsibilities. His words can be analyzed at many different levels and are worthy of such analysis and study. The address represents a distinct communication on the part of the apostle Paul in Acts because he is directly addressing believers in a church that he founded on the occasion of his departure. But at the risk of oversimplification, I want us to view Paul's words as an example and guide for us. Of course, there was a uniqueness to his ministry and to the specific context of ministry in Ephesus. But we can learn from Paul's address and his example.

Read through this inspiring address from beginning to end, keeping in mind the important framework (vv. 17–18, 36–38) and the audience. Put yourself in the shoes (or sandals) of the original hearers as you listen intensely to what the beloved apostle has to say. Let his deep confidence, passion, and integrity inspire you as a leader.

You know, from the first day that I came to Asia, in what manner I always lived among you, serving the Lord with all humility, with many tears and trials which happened to me by the plotting of the Jews; how I kept back nothing that was helpful, but proclaimed it to you, and taught you publicly and from house to house, testifying to Jews, and also to Greeks, repentance toward God and faith toward our Lord Jesus Christ. And see, now I go bound in the spirit to Jerusalem, not knowing the things that will happen to me there, except that the Holy Spirit testifies in every city, saying that chains and tribulations await me.

But none of these things move me; nor do I count my life dear to myself, so that I may finish my race with joy, and the ministry which I received from the Lord Jesus, to testify to the gospel of the grace of God. And indeed, now I know that you all, among whom I have gone preaching the kingdom of God, will see my face no more. Therefore I testify to you this day that I am innocent of the blood of all men. For I have not shunned to declare to you the whole counsel of God.

Therefore take heed to yourselves and to all the flock, among which the Holy Spirit has made you overseers, to shepherd the church of God which He purchased with His own blood. For I know this, that after my departure savage wolves will come in among you, not sparing the flock. Also from among yourselves men will rise up, speaking perverse things, to draw away the disciples after themselves. Therefore watch, and remember that for three years I did not cease to warn everyone night and day with tears.

So now, brethren, I commend you to God and to the word of His grace, which is able to build you up and give you an inheritance among all those who are sanctified. I have coveted no one's silver or gold or apparel. Yes, you yourselves know that these hands have provided for my necessities, and for those who were with me. I have shown you in every way, by laboring like this, that you must support the weak. And remember the words of the Lord Jesus, that He said, "It is more blessed to give than to receive." (Acts 20:18–35)

Over the years I often heard my father say something like this: "God is far more interested in what you are than in what you do." If what we are fails to show forth the example that God wants us to show, then what we do really doesn't matter. This is particularly true for leaders and people in ministry. Paul could say elsewhere, when he directed the Corinthians to follow his example, "Imitate me, just as I also imitate Christ" (1 Cor. 11:1). Paul emphasized this need for exemplary living when he instructed Timothy, "Let no one despise your youth, but be an example to the believers in word, in conduct, in love, in spirit, in faith, in purity" (1 Tim. 4:12). The apostle Paul lived and served in an exemplary manner in Ephesus, and he drew direct attention to this in his address. He left a personal example above reproach that the leaders could remember and seek to follow.

It does not appear from our text that Paul had any major regrets about his life or ministry in Ephesus. Furthermore, he could call the Ephesian elders to account in their knowledge of his life and ministry. Listen to how he began this farewell address. What are the first two words in English? *You know.* "You know," he says, "from the first day that I came to Asia, in what manner I always lived among you" (Acts 20:18). As we near the end of Luke's account of Paul's words, we read, "Yes, you yourselves know" (v. 34), and in verse 35, "I have shown you." In effect, Paul is saying, "I left you an example, and you know that what I am saying is true." Certainly Paul is defending his ministry here, as he did on other occasions. But this motivation of "apologia" does not erase the pastoral and instructive roles of these words.

Characterized by Consistency

"You know, *from the first day* that I came to Asia, in what manner I *always* lived among you" (v. 18, emphasis mine). Paul made plain in these words that there was an ongoing consistency to the way he lived and ministered in Ephesus. He was not controlled by circumstances, people, money, or anything other than the call that God had on his life. He lived and carried out his ministry consistently. He didn't gear up his ministry when people started appreciating him. He didn't try harder when he got a pay raise.

What a need we have for consistency in our lives! How important it is that we live consistently before others, starting with our spouses, our children, and the people whom we are seeking to influence. As a parent, I have seen how frustrating it can be to a child when they see inconsistency in our lives, and especially when what we say doesn't match what we do. Such frustration, though, is not limited to children but can be experienced by anyone who is seeking to follow our leadership or example.

As I think about my own life, I have written down some important words in association with various areas. When it comes to my inner life, the word *discipline* is my main concern. When it comes to marriage, the word *sacrifice* is primary for me. In my involvements with others, I have written down the word *initiative*. In relation to ministry, my key word is *consistency*. Consistency obviously relates to all the other words on my list. Consistency speaks of a lifestyle or a pattern. We all know that it is possible to be consistent in negative ways as well as positive ways. We can be a consistent complainer, a critic, a liar, or something else. We can even be consistently inconsistent! But, of course, Paul is speaking about the consistency of exemplary living and ministry practice that characterized all his days in Ephesus.

Characterized by Humility

What was the manner of Paul's ministry? "Serving the Lord *with all humility*, with many tears and trials which happened to me by the plotting of the Jews" (v. 19, emphasis mine). We know that the apostle Paul had authority, and yet he came as the Lord's servant and he came to serve accordingly. True authority and true humility do not conflict. They exist together. Only as we are serving humbly under the Lord's authority can we exercise the authority He has given us. Paul ministered as a servant, not as a self-seeking kingdom builder. How did humility manifest itself in Paul's life?

PAUL'S SUBMISSION TO HIS LORD

Notice Paul said, "Serving the Lord" (v. 19). That was his agenda—to do what his Lord had called him to do. One of the key ingredients to true humility in the believer's life is to live under lordship, to take all our calls from the Lord, to be about His business, to do His bidding, to do what He calls us to do. You can see Paul's submission to the Lord in verse 19, but also as he talked about what was about to happen in his life. He said, "I go bound in the spirit to Jerusalem, not knowing the things that will happen to me there, except that the Holy Spirit testifies in every city, saying that chains and tribulations await me. But none of these things move me; nor do I count my life dear to myself" (vv. 22–24). Why would Paul say that? Disregarding the prophecies of suffering that he knew he was going to face, he says, "So that I may finish my race with joy, and the ministry which I received from the Lord Jesus, to testify to the gospel of the grace of God" (v. 24). Paul received his ministry from the Lord and therefore he was to do what the Lord called him to do. What allegiance! What loyalty! What a sense of direct accountability and responsibility!

People can be controlled by allegiances and loyalties other than the Lord that can deflect from the directness and the dynamic of living in total submission, surrender, and obedience to Him. Ultimately, it is because of our submission to the Lord that we submit to whom and to what the Lord directs us. Such humility and submission are to be genuine, but they flow from the prior and primary submission to Christ. To state this in a radical way, there is a sense in which we are free from every human authority, except those we are called to submit to "for the Lord's sake" (1 Pet. 2:13). Every act or posture of submission in our lives is to be the outflow of our submission to the Lord—the *expression* of our submission to the Lord. Don't miss this! We express humility in our lives and service when we choose to submit to others (and to other "ordinances") as the Lord directs. This relates to marriage, the family, church life, work responsibilities, relationships, community involvements, our citizenship, and our response to civil and governmental authorities.

PAUL'S SUFFERING FOR THE LORD

Not only do we see Paul's humility in his *submission* to the Lord; we see it in his *suffering*. "Serving the Lord with all humility, with many tears and trials which happened to me by the plotting of the Jews" (Acts 20:19). Paul could have said, "Hey, I'm outta here. I don't need to deal with this opposition." But he accepted suffering as a cost of ministry.

Humility and servanthood are demonstrated in suffering, as we see in the life of our Lord Jesus Christ. In Philippians 2:5 and following, Paul talked about having the same mind of selflessness and humility which were in Christ Jesus. Christ Jesus mysteriously and wonderfully let go of His divine prerogatives, came to earth, took upon Himself the form of a servant, and went to the cross. This passage speaks of our Lord humbling Himself, becoming "obedient to the point of death, even the death of the cross" (v. 8). This involved real suffering.

Paul suffered much throughout his ministry, and such was the case in Ephesus: "tears and trials." He lived and served with the knowledge that there were those who were out to "get him." And "get him" didn't just mean to get him out of the church; they wanted him out of town, indeed out of sight completely. This was the backdrop of Paul's life.

Living and serving with suffering is a true mark of humility. We will touch on this subject of suffering again later in our study, but it is fair to ask, what are we willing to face or to suffer in our service for the Lord? Suffering is part of the job description of the Christian and the leader especially. It should not surprise us nor deflect us from serving the Lord. I am not saying we should be foolish or reckless in our approach to suffering. Paul fled persecution at times, and he used his Roman citizenship to avoid suffering. But opposition or suffering itself is not to be the deciding factor in one's ministry responsibilities. God may use such circumstances to open up new doors of service or to move us on, but He may also use such circumstances to shape us and to purify our lives and ministries. Are we willing to suffer if we are called to do so? That is a test, indeed, a *mark* of humility.

I am so thankful to God that I have had the privilege of ministering with and to many brothers and sisters in Christ in other countries. For me to even speak of suffering on my part is almost blasphemy. Praise God for the countless faithful servants of the Lord who live and serve faithfully in the context of suffering regularly, if not daily. We need to examine our own hearts to see how often we make decisions to stop ministry or to leave places of service just to avoid hardship or loss, to avoid "tears and trials," to distance ourselves from the schemes and plots of unbelievers and others. Again, I am not advocating stupidity, but I am saying we follow a Lord whose ministry involved suffering. I am saying that we can expect suffering. I am saying that God uses suffering to further His purposes in our lives and in our ministries. I am saying that we need to serve humbly where we are, allowing the Lord to clearly lead us to other places of service if that is His desire. But here in this text, we learn that Paul suffered for the Lord as he was doing ministry.

Paul's suffering was due to direct plotting and persecution. As I have referred to previously, there are many faithful servants of the Lord in our world today who are facing tremendous hardship, threats, dangers, and direct persecution. But even in contexts where direct physical persecution is not a daily reality, many servants of the Lord face everything from resistance to direct confrontation in their ministries. I suppose I have almost heard it all working with pastors and church leaders over the past twenty-plus years. Ministry comes at a cost. Ministry involves pain, and there is probably no pain like "people pain." Humility is challenged when we face people who question, people who argue, people who threaten, people who sin against us, people who seek to hinder authentic ministry. Humility is likewise challenged as we engage a culture that criticizes and even condemns certain beliefs, practices, and ministries that are essential to biblical Christianity. Having the "mind" of Christ in these situations is a true test of humility. Such humility will result in allegiance and obedience to the Lord and His will, even in the midst of opposition. Such humility will result in service of others, even when criticized and misunderstood.

Paul's Support of the Weak

Paul said at the end of this speech, "You yourselves know that these hands have provided for my necessities, and for those who were with me. I have shown you in every way, by laboring like this, that you must support the weak" (Acts 20:34–35). Paul does not relate these comments directly to humility, but I want to suggest that these comments are another evidence of genuine humility in his life. Paul wasn't so big that he lorded over people or took advantage of people—exactly the opposite! He worked with his hands so that he could provide for himself and those with him. Paul was leaving an example to the Ephesian leaders concerning support for the "weak."

How a person relates to the needy, weak, vulnerable—indeed all those who need help— will indicate whether or not he or she is a person of humility. Paul did not want to be a burden on the people with whom and to whom he ministered. His ministry was to the weak, to those who could not or did not give back in full. Does this not bring to mind the teachings of Jesus, indeed the life of Jesus? He was the anointed one who, in keeping with His Messianic role, was sent to "preach the gospel to the poor . . . heal the broken hearted . . . proclaim liberty to the captives and recovery of sight to the blind, to set at liberty those who are oppressed; to proclaim the acceptable year of the Lord" (Luke 4:18–19; Isa. 61:1–2).

Humility means that we are willing to do what is necessary to serve others, especially those who are not in a position to repay. It is easy to become demanding in ministry when we really think we are *somebody*! I am not talking about the need for churches, ministries, institutions, or businesses to do what is right in terms of compensation for services rendered. That is another issue. But Paul was not driven by financial gain, nor did the money issue keep him from the ministry God called him to do. Humility expresses itself in not coveting gain or financial advantage. We will look at the integrity issue shortly, but here we make the connection between Paul's "serving the Lord with *all humility*" (Acts 20:19, emphasis mine), and his example of working with his hands in order to provide for himself and others.

F. F. Bruce points out the emphatic position of the phrase "these hands" (v. 34), suggesting that Paul's words "were no doubt accompanied by an appropriate gesture."[3] I know we are only speculating or using our imaginations, but don't you think it is possible that Paul drew attention to his own hands as he said these words? He was willing to do the manual work necessary to fund the ministry. He used his hands, his own hands, "these hands." One wonders what those hands must have looked like.

I'm sure they visibly demonstrated the results of manual labor. Remember, we are talking about being an example, specifically an example of humility. Paul was a visual aid for how these leaders were to help those in need—the weak—those who didn't have much to give.

Let's be honest in answering this question: How do we conduct ourselves in relation to others? Are we always hoping to be recognized? Do we want to be served rather than serve? Do we complain when we suffer? Do we refuse to do extra work to help others? Do we get tired of helping the weak and the needy? How we answer these questions will give an indication of whether or not we are really marked with humility. *Humility* is a word that is thrown around without meaningful or practical content at times. Paul gives us content to consider as we look at his example. He served the Lord. He suffered with tears and trials. He chose to work manually to provide for himself and others, helping the weak.

Characterized by Intensity

As we read these verses, we get a tremendous sense of focus. You get the impression that Paul was active; indeed, this man was driven. Paul wasn't in ministry for what he could get out of it; he was in it because he had a call from God. He talked about "how I kept back nothing that was helpful, but proclaimed it to you, and taught you publicly and from house to house, testifying to Jews, and also to Greeks, repentance toward God and faith toward our Lord Jesus Christ" (vv. 20–21).

Later as Paul revealed his future plans, he said that none of the possibilities of suffering moved him; in essence, they were not going to keep him from finishing his race with joy, and completing his ministry (v. 24). He had an intense passion and sense of commitment to complete what he was called to do. Looking back at his time of ministry in Ephesus, Paul brings to his listeners' remembrance "that for three years I did not cease to warn everyone night and day with tears" (v. 31). This was a full and intense ministry. "Night and day with tears" (v. 31). There was emotional intensity. There was ministerial intensity. As we would say today, he gave everything he had. He didn't hold back anything. He proclaimed everything profitable. He taught publicly. He went house to house. He ministered to Jews. He ministered to Greeks. There was an intensity to Paul's life and ministry due to his commitment to what the Lord had called him to do. Paul would go anywhere and say what needed to be said, and he did it "night and day." You don't get the sense that Paul was tied to a narrow job description or to an eight-hour day.

How easy it is to get off track. It's easy to lose focus, to give up, to hold back, and not give all. We should have a driving motivation to be doing what God has called us to do. If God has called us to be a parent, then we should parent with that same kind of intensity, concern, and focus for our children. If there is a Sunday school class, a church ministry, or some organization that God has given us responsibility over, we should demonstrate an intense concern to serve in this role. We must look at the circle of influence that God has given us, and we must do what God has called us to do with God-glorifying intensity.

As we look at this passage, we see a man who gave it all he had. Paul held back nothing in life, in word, or in ministry. Personally and ministerially, he was "in it." This characteristic of intensity was part of the example he displayed in Ephesus, and it was part of what Paul wanted these leaders to remember.

Characterized by Accountability

Paul also had a great sense of accountability. He was accountable to the Lord and accountable to the Word. As he talked about what was ahead, he spoke of the need to fulfill what the Lord Jesus had called him to do:

> And see, now I go bound in the spirit to Jerusalem, not knowing the things that will happen to me there, except that the Holy Spirit testifies in every city, saying that chains and tribulations await me. But none of these things move me; nor do I count my

life dear to myself, so that I may finish my race with joy, and the ministry which I received from the Lord Jesus, to testify to the gospel of the grace of God. (Acts 20:22–24)

The apostle Paul believed that he had "received" his ministry "from the Lord Jesus" (v. 24). He was not simply pursuing a career that he had chosen personally for himself. He believed that the Lord had met him, called him, and graced him to be the apostle to the Gentiles and to testify "to the gospel of the grace of God" (v. 24). Paul came to Ephesus because he was led of the Lord. He served the Lord in Ephesus, and his life's ambition was to fulfill the ministry the Lord had given him to do.

I remember a past member of our ministry staff saying that he believed in "received ministry." I know this phrase didn't originate with him, but it struck me when he said it. What does "received ministry" mean? It means that ministry is not something we just decide to do and then simply try to accomplish for God. No, ministry is something God calls us to do, gives us to do, and then does through us as we serve Him. So whatever we do in ministry or wherever it is exercised, ultimately we are accountable to the Lord as well as dependent upon Him. Paul believed this. As we will see later, Paul certainly believed that the Lord had authorized him for ministry (Rom. 1:1–7; 15:15–16), and his boast was what Christ did through him (15:18). For Paul, this meant that the opinions and the judgments of men were not final; it was the judgment of the Lord that counted (1 Cor. 4:1–4). He lived with a sense of accountability to his Lord.

I have always enjoyed reading the words of exhortation near the end of Paul's epistle to the Colossians. We read, "And say to Archippus, 'Take heed to the ministry which you have received in the Lord, that you may fulfill it'" (Col. 4:17). Here Paul directs the church at Colosse to exhort this man, possibly the same person mentioned in Philemon 2, to fulfill his ministry. But note the phrase "the ministry which you have received in the Lord." Paul wanted Archippus to understand that doing this ministry task (whatever it was) was something that needed to be done with an awareness of the ultimate source of his ministry, the Lord Himself. The responsibility was granted by the Lord, and to the Lord he was accountable. This is true for all of us. Such a sense of responsibility and accountability should help to remind us that we are first and foremost to be faithful to the Lord in all things.

It is worth noting as well the specific accountability to the Word of God that Paul sensed. Look at the following verses: "And indeed, now I know that you all, among whom I have gone preaching the kingdom of God, will see my face no more. Therefore I testify to you this day that I am innocent of the blood of all men. For I have not shunned to declare to you the whole counsel of God" (Acts 20:25–27).

Paul had a sense of accountability to the message that the Lord had given him to deliver. He was not necessarily talking about having preached on every single verse in the Old Testament. In effect he was saying, "I have not held back declaring the gospel. I have not held back in declaring the whole counsel, the revelation that the Lord has given me to proclaim. I have been faithful. I have not been negligent, deceptive, or selective. I have preached all that the Lord has called me to preach." He held back nothing. This is exemplary for us who have the task of preaching or teaching the Word of God today. We will look at this more thoroughly in our next chapter.

Characterized by Integrity

Before we leave this matter of Paul's example, we need to consider a characteristic that is essential for effective leadership and service—*integrity*. Integrity has to do with being true to who we are and to our real principles. It has to do with an agreement between one's personal beliefs and his behavior. Integrity involves having pure motives and methods, being honest at the deepest level. How was Paul's integrity demonstrated in this text?

He didn't use the exact word—"integrity"—but the very way in which he reminded the Ephesian leaders of his ministry indicated he was defending his integrity. Paul even states that he had not coveted material possessions: "I have coveted no one's silver or gold or apparel" (v. 33). In fact, he labored to meet his own financial needs and those of others ministering. Why would he say that? Why would he even point to that? Paul was reminding the Ephesian leaders of his pure motives in ministry. Paul came to serve the Lord. He came to fulfill his ministry. His motivation inside matched his ministry outside. He was not hiding anything. He came to serve the Lord, to preach the Word, to strengthen the people, and to fulfill the ministry. He wasn't discouraged or defeated by suffering, nor distracted by possible personal gain. He did not have selfish or sinful motivation in his ministry.

We live in a world that desperately needs models of integrity. It is not assumed that leaders have integrity. As a matter of fact, there is great distrust toward leaders today. We hear people talk about leaders in ways that indicate, "We just assume there is something under the table. We assume a hidden agenda. We assume there is something wrong. We assume a lack of integrity." Why? Because so often this proves to be the case. When things are exposed and made known, we discover moral or financial scandals. People build their own kingdoms or do things on the side or underneath that really have nothing to do with—and indeed negate—the ministry or service of the individual. Integrity has to be demonstrated in our day. It cannot be assumed. What we leave behind needs to indicate that while we were there, in that position, in that place, we lived with integrity. Paul is really saying, "I have shown you that I have lived and operated with integrity."

What a legacy to leave behind, a personal example that people can look to, be blessed by, and indeed follow! We need to consider this example of the apostle Paul and reflect on it: consistency, humility, intensity, accountability, integrity.

What strikes me, as I reflect on these aspects of Paul's address, is the amount of time Paul gave to defend his manner of ministry. How he lived and served were critically important to him. His example became a lasting legacy of his days in Ephesus, one that the leaders of the church of Ephesus would remember. What do we want people to remember about us? What *will* they remember about us? Faithfulness involves leaving a personal example that others will be able to follow. "Oh, may all who come behind us find us faithful."[4]

CHAPTER 2

The Legacy of a Preached Word

A major subject that received attention in Paul's address was his ministry of the Word. This was a priority in terms of Paul's mission, goals, and activities while in Ephesus. This certainly should not be a surprise to us, since the apostle Paul identified the ministry he "received from the Lord Jesus" as being "to testify to the gospel of the grace of God" (Acts 20:24). Therefore, you would expect that Paul would say a lot about his communication of the gospel and the Word of God in this farewell address, and he did.

One potential weakness in ministry practice is to allow the various demands of ministry to crowd out the priority need of communicating God's truth. The apostle Paul embraced the responsibility of communicating divine revelation as fundamental and foremost in his apostolic ministry. A major concern in his ministry was to proclaim God's truth faithfully, knowing that this "Word" would be the basis for church health and growth after his departure.

In this chapter we will be looking at what Paul preached and taught at Ephesus. More than leaving behind a personal example to remember, Paul left God's Word, which would sustain the believers and help them grow. This was fundamental to being faithful as a leader and as a preacher of "the gospel of the grace of God" (v. 24).

It is safe to say that Paul preached the Word at Ephesus without reserve. He did not hold back. "I kept back nothing that was helpful," he said (v. 20). Where did Paul communicate his teaching and message?

He taught, he preached, he proclaimed publicly and from house to house. The picture here is not of a set number of formal speaking occasions on a church calendar. It is the picture of a passionate communicator speaking on numerous different occasions, whenever and wherever possible. There was the open public ministry of the Word, and there were the smaller settings, from house to house. To whom did Paul minister? "To Jews, and also to Greeks" (v. 21), which speaks of the fact that Paul didn't limit his audience. Some details from Acts 19 will help us here. The narrative tells us that when Paul was in Ephesus:

> He went into the synagogue and spoke boldly for three months, reasoning and persuading concerning the things of the kingdom of God. But when some were hardened and did not believe, but spoke evil of the Way before the multitude, he departed from them and withdrew the disciples, reasoning daily in the school of Tyrannus. And this continued for two years, so that all who dwelt in Asia heard the word of the Lord Jesus, both Jews and Greeks. (Acts 19:8–10)

Paul's pattern was to start in the Jewish context and to proceed according to what happened. His strategy seemed to follow his understanding of revelation and salvation history (Rom. 1:16; 11:1–33). Even at the end of Luke's account, when Paul arrived at Rome, it appears that he met with the Jewish leaders first (Acts 28:17). Granted, he was a prisoner and wanted to explain his situation, but Luke's account ends with this same pattern. Even though Paul saw himself as an apostle to the nations (Rom. 1:5; 15:15–21), he did not forget his own people nor ignore their historical and theological place and privilege. But Paul's ultimate goal was to preach to the nations (plural). And that he did! Luke ends his account by recording that, despite Paul's circumstances, he "dwelt two whole years in his own rented house, and received all who came to him, preaching the kingdom of God and teaching the things which concern the Lord Jesus Christ with all confidence, no one forbidding him"

(Acts 28:30–31). Certainly one theme in Luke's account is the spreading of the Word of God, and the account ends with the irony of the unfettered Word being declared by a prisoner in Rome! But our main observation here is that Paul communicated his message to both Jews and Greeks.

How did Paul communicate his message? The words Luke used in Acts 20 (in English) are *proclaim, teach, testify, preach, declare,* and *warn.* We also see the words *reasoning* and *persuading* in the Acts 19 account (v. 8). These words reveal that Paul communicated his message in a variety of ways and contexts. It would be hard to defend one style of presentation from these words, and that is instructive in and of itself. Paul ministered in various settings, to various people, and with various emphases. His passion and commitment to proclaim God's truth is what resulted in the extensive vocabulary needed to describe his ministry of the Word in Ephesus.

To learn from Paul's example, I'd like us to consider his communication of the Word of God under some broad categories. We'll speak of what he left behind at Ephesus as his "preached Word"—what he actually communicated of God's truth. And as we think about this preached Word that he left behind at Ephesus, we will describe it in a three-fold manner: an *evangelistic* Word, a *comprehensive* Word, and a *powerful* Word. Certainly this is a model for us as we think about church planting and local church ministry, as well as communicating the Word of God in general.

An Evangelistic Word

Paul preached the gospel. Three references are made in Paul's speech to the gospel and those truths that specifically relate to the gospel of our Lord and Savior Jesus Christ. In Acts 20:21, Paul says that he testified "to Jews, and also to Greeks, repentance toward God and faith toward our Lord Jesus Christ." Paul summarized his message to Jews and to Greeks in this fashion. Paul's preaching was certainly both theological and Christological. He communicated truths about God and the Lord Jesus

Christ, as the text states here. But his message also clearly expressed the need for response on the part of his audience in terms of "repentance" and "faith."

For example, Paul's message to the Athenians emphasized "repentance" in the light of pending judgment through the Resurrected One (Acts 17:30–31). Such repentance involved turning from their idolatry and ignorance to the living Creator God, and the time for such a response was "now." To the Jews and God-fearers in the synagogue in Antioch (Pisidia), the thrust was the need for belief: "By Him [Jesus] everyone who believes is justified from all things from which you could not be justified by the law of Moses" (Acts 13:39). Forgiveness and justification were preached and were to be experienced through faith in Jesus Christ rather than through works of the Law.

These two messages of Paul illustrate his preaching in Jewish and Gentile contexts, but it is not necessary to assume that repentance was the only thing needed by the Gentiles, or that faith was the only thing needed by the Jews. I don't think these two examples should limit our understanding of these two critical phrases in Acts 20:21. Rather, I think it is appropriate to interpret Paul's description of his message in verse 21 as summarizing the core truths and issues that were at the heart of his evangelistic communication.

In vers 24, Paul speaks of testifying "to the gospel of the grace of God." Paul viewed this as being at the heart of his ministry received from the Lord. We know how important the word "grace" was to Paul. Grace was foundational and fundamental to Paul's understanding of his own life. God called Paul out of the life he was living and called him to Himself. God called him into the ministry and called him as an apostle. Paul knew grace personally in his own life, and he knew the revealed message of grace. Indeed this was how he characterized the gospel itself. The gospel was and is the gospel of the grace of God. The gospel is about what God has done in Christ to bring about a necessary salvation to all who believe. This provision is in and through Christ and it is provided freely by grace alone, through faith alone. Men and women who are dead in sin and trespasses, condemned under the righteous law of God and subject to God's wrath, are desperately in need of salvation. Indeed, outside of God's provision in Christ, they are helpless and hopeless. But God, in grace, has broken into this helpless and hopeless situation by sending His own Son to die a death "for our sins," a substitutionary death that was a sacrifice for sin, so that forgiveness could become a reality (1 Cor. 15:3–5). Through repentance and faith, justification and forgiveness are appropriated, and a right relationship with God is established. And we have only started to expound some of the main Pauline themes in the gospel of the grace of God.[1]

Paul, in Acts 20:25, said something else about his apostolic message. He spoke of "preaching the kingdom of God." This reminds us of one of the main themes in Jesus' preaching and teaching ministry—the reign and rule of God. This "kingdom" message was one that Paul presented also, in continuity with Jesus' preaching, but it expounds the person and work of Christ from this side of the cross and resurrection.

So what have we seen? Paul's gospel called for response—repentance and faith. His gospel expounded the grace of God. Furthermore, He preached the *kingdom* of God. He preached these essentials clearly and powerfully.

Today we need a clear evangelistic message. People need to hear the gospel. Those who do not know our Lord and Savior Jesus Christ need to hear the Word of grace, the Word of salvation. Not only do nonbelievers need to hear the gospel, young Christians need to hear and learn more about the gospel in order to be established in it. Older Christians need to be reminded of the gospel regularly, which will increase their awareness and appreciation of gospel truths. We should never get too used to the grace of God. The grace that saved us is the same grace that sustains us and sees us through to the end. We should never "get over" the gospel. We need to be passionate about the gospel. We should seek to declare and teach the gospel through whatever avenues are available.

We know there is a core to the gospel—Jesus Christ and Him crucified—His death, burial, resurrection, and post-resurrection appearances

(1 Cor. 15:1–11). But around this core are related truths that need to be declared to explain the events that happened so many years ago through our Lord Jesus. Yes, the facts of history are fundamental to the gospel message. But those facts need to be seen in the light of who Christ is and what God accomplished in and through His Son.

The Roman epistle is a greatly expanded statement of the gospel presented instructively and apologetically. But it would take a study of the rest of the New Testament and the Old Testament to see the truths of the gospel in all their fullness, a fullness of grace and glory. We don't need to reduce the gospel to the bare minimum; rather we should connect the scriptural dots for people.[2] We need to proclaim the big picture of God's purpose, plan, and provision involving His Son and the Holy Spirit in bringing about our salvation—past, present, and future. We have an eternal message, rich and diverse in both its implications and applications. Although Paul could reduce his message to one word in English—"Him"—the ripples from this magnificent, mysterious gospel move onward and outward.

The Comprehensive Word

Paul definitely preached the gospel, the evangelistic Word. But he made a statement in the middle of his address that needs special attention as we consider the message he left behind in Ephesus: "Therefore I testify to you this day that I am innocent of the blood of all men" (Acts 20:26). Why could Paul say that? "For I have not shunned to declare to you the whole counsel of God" (v. 27). He had already said, in verse 20, that he had kept back nothing that was helpful but proclaimed it to these people and taught them publicly and from house to house. Here we have an insight into Paul's concern to preach the Word comprehensively. What was he saying? He was claiming innocence. He declared that he was not responsible for the lives and deaths of the people to whom he ministered. Why? Because he had proclaimed the *whole* counsel, the *whole* will, the *whole* purpose of God. Paul had not been selective, deceptive, or negligent in the preaching and teaching ministry that he exercised. God had set the agenda for Paul's ministry and message. Paul was saying that like Ezekiel's watchman of old (Ezek. 33:1–9), he had been faithful to communicate the necessary message.[3]

It is the responsibility of the preacher to pass on the message that God has revealed—that God has declared—and this is exactly what Paul said he had done. He was saying that he had been faithful in preaching. That is why I use the word "comprehensive." He preached the gospel— the clear gospel, the full gospel. He preached it conscientiously, edifying and strengthening the people in Ephesus. As Paul went around Ephesus and was involved in ministry, his passion was to declare not only the core of the gospel but the Word that would be profitable, the Word that would be helpful to the growth of the church. This commitment to faithfulness in his message—a sense of accountability to the Lord and to the Word— drove Paul in his ministry. What a word to us today! This needs to be our concern as servants of the Lord—to do what He tells us to do and to preach the message He calls us to preach. Paul wasn't saying that he specifically preached Genesis 1:1 through Malachi 4:4, verse-by-verse, day-by-day. Paul may have covered the Old Testament in one way or another or summarized the Old Testament teachings as they related to Christ. We don't know exactly what he taught from the Scriptures day in and day out in Ephesus. But what we do know is that God had revealed the gospel to Paul as a chosen apostle, and he sought to declare that revelation faithfully.

How do we relate this to our lives today? We have the completed canon of Scripture—sixty-six books that contain the inspired, inerrant Word of God. This completed canon of Scripture bears witness to our Lord Jesus Christ and to the saving gospel we need to declare. We need to be faithful to this book. We need to preach it in a way that covers the truths of this book and seeks to be faithful to what God has revealed of Himself. At the center of our message needs to be Christ Himself, who is the Living Word. Around "Him" are the truths that help explain His person and work. Furthermore, throughout the Scriptures are the broader truths that God has revealed for His people to know and to live. Such Scriptures "are able to make [one] wise for salvation through faith which is in Christ Jesus" (2 Tim. 3:15). But Paul affirmed the significance of all Scripture by saying that "all Scripture is given by inspiration of God, and is profitable for doctrine, for reproof, for correction, for instruction in righteousness, that the man of God may be complete, thoroughly equipped for every good work" (vv. 16–17). We know that Paul was speaking of the Old Testament Scriptures in 2 Timothy, but these statements are also valid for the New Testament Scriptures as well. So we have a completed canon of Scripture that is profitable to lead people to salvation in Christ and to help them grow into maturity in Christ. To this Word we must be faithful.

On a practical level, many approaches may be suggested to enable a preacher to be faithful to the "whole counsel of God" (Acts 20:27). We need not be legalistic in presenting one approach for all. But why not think about an approach that enables the preacher or teacher to move through the Scriptures in some manner? This does not necessitate teaching verse-by-verse from Genesis 1:1 through Revelation 22:21, although this is certainly a long-range possibility. What I am encouraging is a commitment to preach and teach Christ and the gospel, "the faith which was once for all delivered to the saints" (Jude 3), the fundamental doctrines and duties for Christian belief and behavior, and a commitment to expose people to the breadth and depth of Scripture. Whatever approach to preaching and teaching is adopted, it should be adopted intentionally with a commitment "to declare . . . the whole counsel of God" (Acts 20:27).

Obviously an evangelist's focus in preaching may be narrower than a pastor or teacher in an established church. But the evangelist needs to be challenged by the apostle's sense of accountability to the Lord and the Word in the presentation of the gospel. The gospel needs to be preached both clearly and comprehensively. Preaching a "simple gospel" does not mean preaching a partial or incomplete gospel. Here I am not so much concerned with an individual message as I am with the character and content of the evangelist's ministry over a period of time. There is no freedom to be deceptive or negligent in presenting the truth of the gospel.

A Powerful Word

Paul left at Ephesus a constructive word to build up the people of God—a word that continues to edify the church in Paul's absence. Remember, Paul was about to leave these leaders. He reminded them, "You're not going to see my face anymore." To what were they going to look to sustain them, to guide them, to direct them, to know God's will for their lives? They had his personal example to which they could look, but they needed the Word of God. They needed the Word to guide them and build them up, to keep them on the right track. He refers to this Word in verse 32 as he commends these leaders to God, "So now, brethren, I commend you to God and to the word of His grace, which is able to build you up and give you an inheritance among all those who are sanctified." In encouraging them, he encourages us that it is the Word which can build us up and sustain us, to "grow us" as believers. God and His Word will see us through to the end, to the time when we gain our inheritance. Praise God for the power of His Word!

The Word of God is able. The Word of God is profitable. The Word of God strengthens and builds up and matures. That's why in our ministries, for those involved in preaching and teaching the Word of God, we do not need to hold back. We have a wonderful Word. We have a powerful Word. We have a Word that makes a difference in people's lives.

How we need to have confidence in the Word of God. God uses His Word by the power of the Holy Spirit. The communicating of the Word of God must be a primary concern in our ministry context. The Ephesian elders were not going to see Paul again. Who were they going to depend on for their future growth? Who or what was going to help them fulfill their responsibilities as believers and leaders? How were they going to do the job they were called to do? A wonderful legacy of Paul's ministry was the faithful proclamation of the Word. Three years, he said, night and day, he did not cease to warn them with tears. He preached the gospel. He preached everything that would edify. He preached the whole counsel of God. Such a commitment needs to be at the core of our understanding and practice of ministry.

I spent most of my boyhood days in the New York area. My father was pastor of Calvary Baptist Church in New York City at that time (1959–1973). I remember an elderly gentleman by the name of Ellsworth Jenkins who taught a Sunday school class when I was a boy. As I look back on that time of training and teaching, I don't remember the specific lessons he taught, but what I do remember is that this man had a love of the Word of God and he encouraged us to study the Bible. I praise God for the legacy he left to me because his love of Scripture was contagious. I can still picture that class and the way he motivated us to get into the Word of God. We need to do that with those who are around us. We need to point them to the Book, to get them into the Word. We need to encourage them to go to the Word of God themselves.

As I think about my father's ministry at Calvary Baptist Church, the same can be said that I shared about Ellsworth Jenkins. The primary activity in the life of the church was the preaching and teaching of the Word of God. Due to the radio ministry at that time, the church walls did not contain the preaching ministry; it went around the world. Hundreds and hundreds of people were saved and built up through this evangelistic, comprehensive, and powerful Word.

In the years after the pastoral ministry that God gave my father, he devoted himself to encouraging pastors, preachers, and teachers to rightly divide the Word of truth (2 Tim. 2:15). This was done by my father with the same type of conviction and passion that characterized the apostle Paul in his "farewell address." He believed in the evangelistic Word and preached it. He had a burden for the faithful proclamation of the Scriptures—that pastors would preach the "whole counsel of God." But fundamental to these convictions was the confidence in the power of the Word of God to do what God desired it to do.

We ended my father's memorial service by playing a brief clip from one of his messages. In the message, he referred to Isaiah 55:10–11:

> For as the rain comes down, and the snow from heaven, and do not return there, but water the earth, and make it bring forth and bud, that it may give seed to the sower and bread to the eater, so shall My word be that goes forth from My mouth; it shall not return to Me void, but it shall accomplish what I please, and it shall prosper in the thing for which I sent it.

This great truth concerning the accomplishing power of the Word of God was what my father said gave him confidence and joy in preaching. Surely this is why we can have confidence when we communicate God's Word. Such confidence is not in ourselves or in our own ability. Our confidence is in the Word of God itself and what God will do with it. Our job is to "rightly divide the Word of truth" in the power of the Holy Spirit.

Is that a part of the legacy we are leaving behind to those around us? We need to point to the Word of God so that they will go to the Word in our absence.

There are two ladies, now gone to be with the Lord, who over the years have been real heroes to the Olford family. These two ladies served the Lord in missionary work in Africa for many years. For approximately twenty of those years, they were in the southern Sudan. Mary Beam and Betty Cridland faced all sorts of challenges and hardships during that time of ministry, and eventually they had to leave the Sudan. Amazingly the newly translated New Testament (along with parts of the Old Testament, I believe) arrived just as they were about to depart. As they were forced to leave the Sudan, they literally left behind the Word of God! What a picture of what we need to do in ministry.

God will call us to move on in His purpose, and God may call us home to be with Himself. But we need to leave behind the Word. It needs to be seen in our lives through our personal example and to be shared from our lips. This is our responsibility. This needs to be our concern. We need to leave the Word of God behind because it is powerful. It does the job. It leads people to salvation through faith in Christ. It brings people into maturity. It builds people up and leads them to the inheritance that is theirs in Christ Jesus.

CHAPTER 3
The Legacy of a Prepared Leadership

Before we focus on another legacy of Paul's ministry, read Luke's simple but powerful narrative of Paul's departure:

And when he had said these things, he knelt down and prayed with them all. Then they all wept freely, and fell on Paul's neck and kissed him, sorrowing most of all for the words which he spoke, that they would see his face no more. And they accompanied him to the ship. (Acts 20:36–38)

Paul was now on his way to Jerusalem, not knowing what would happen to him. We know from history that Paul went through a variety of difficult experiences before he eventually ended up in Rome. But here in Acts 20, we have this scene filled with dynamism and emotion. Paul was leaving people who meant much to him. Paul had literally given himself in ministry in Ephesus. He had left behind a personal example above reproach that the people could remember and follow. He had left behind a preached Word that would build them up in the future. But a third legacy of Paul's ministry was a *prepared leadership*.

What does leaving behind a "prepared leadership" mean for you and me? It means we need to be in the business of influencing others, both modeling and helping others grow in Christ. We are to enable others to take up where we leave off. We need to multiply ourselves in the lives of others. That's what Paul did.

Luke records for us in Acts 14:23 that during Paul's first missionary journey, he appointed elders in every church. The general pattern seemed to be as follows: the gospel was preached, people became disciples, these disciples were "strengthened," and leaders were appointed. Later Paul would write concerning the qualifications of such leaders in 1 Timothy 3 and Titus 1. Here in Acts 20, we have a record of Paul's charge to these leaders who had already been selected but now were facing a new phase of ministry in light of the apostle's departure. As we look at Acts 20, we are going to see how these leaders were prepared for Paul's departure.

An Instructed Leadership

Paul referred to three years of ministry, of warnings that the elders could remember. "Remember," he says, "that for three years I did not cease to warn everyone night and day with tears" (v. 31). This doesn't mean that these leaders were there during every one of those ministry occasions, but they were people who had been influenced by Paul's passionate communication of truth. Much of Paul's ministry would have been exercised to larger groups, but these elders—these leaders—were aware of it. Along the way Paul had taught them, probably in both formal and informal settings. Paul taught them the Word of God, as we saw in the previous chapter. Paul taught them by his personal example, as we saw in chapter 1. He could make such a statement as, "I have coveted no one's silver or gold or apparel. Yes, you yourselves know that these hands have provided for my necessities. . . . I have shown you in every way, by laboring like this, that you must support the weak" (vv. 33–35). Paul trained these leaders by drawing attention to his personal practice and approach to ministry.

Leaders need to be trained. People need to be trained to deal with life, to deal with any position of responsibility. That takes time. And it takes time to communicate the truth of the Word of God and to show that truth in our lives. This leadership at Ephesus was aware of the Word of God. They were a leadership that had an example to follow. They had been instructed.

It is interesting that Paul specifically reminds them of his warnings "with tears" (v. 31). As leaders they were to "watch." They were to "take heed to [themselves] and to all the flock . . . to shepherd the church of God" (v. 28). Much of this ministry would be that of vigilant watching and caring for the people of God. Paul's years of ministry and especially his warnings and admonishments would need to be remembered. Their task was not going to be easy, and they needed to recognize the seriousness of the challenge and the responsibility.

It is very dangerous when people are appointed to positions of responsibility with little or no training and preparation. Paul's farewell address indicates these leaders were aware of Paul's manner of life and ministry as well as the Word he proclaimed. They had been instructed in ways that would prepare them for the role of "watchers," overseers of the people of God.

An Appointed Leadership

Listen to these words: "Take heed to yourselves and to all the flock, among which the Holy Spirit has made you overseers, to shepherd the church of God which He purchased with His own blood" (v. 28). Paul attributes to the Holy Spirit the role of appointing leaders. It is the Holy Spirit who gives gifts and ministry to the local church. It is with the guidance of the Holy Spirit that we can discern those who are to function in terms of their gifts and in terms of leadership. At some point these people were specifically appointed in a way that was recognized by the church. Indeed that was Paul's standard practice, as we referred to in Acts 14:23.

In the Pastoral Epistles we learn about the characteristics, qualifications, and ministries of such leaders. But the actual process of appointing leaders is not spelled out for all time. We have insight into Timothy's possible "appointment," when Paul told Timothy not to neglect the gift that had been given to him "by prophecy with the laying on of the hands of the eldership" (1 Tim. 4:14). This matter of acknowledging leadership—of people being gifted, appointed, and recognized—was something important in the life of the early church.

There comes a time when the role of leadership doesn't need to be vague. It doesn't need to be something slipped into or treated casually. There should be a time of recognition, an appointment. It must be of God and through the Holy Spirit. And it ought to be done meaningfully and prayerfully, within a ministry organization or within the life of the church. Paul could say, as he spoke to these elders, "Take heed to yourselves and to all the flock, among which the Holy Spirit has made you overseers" (Acts 20:28). The very fact that Paul had called for these elders and that they had come to him as a group indicates they were a recognized group of leaders. So leaders not only need to be instructed, they need to be appointed and, in that sense, affirmed in the position God has given them. Paul attributes this appointment to the Holy Spirit. The appointment was not simply by the apostle himself or some human agency or decision. Certainly there would have been people involved, but Paul does not emphasize the human element. What he emphasizes is the role of the Holy Spirit.

It is sad to say, but many would be cynical toward such a statement being made concerning leadership today. First of all, how the Holy Spirit actually leads in such matters may not even be discussed. People may be scared to attribute Holy Spirit "authority" to leaders, since it is easier to deal with "elected officials." There may be some people, of course, who believe that the way Paul did it died with him since he was an apostle. My concern here is not to go deeper into matters that are left in the background of New Testament practice. What I do want to stress, though, is the straightforward way Paul speaks of the Holy Spirit's role in the leader's appointment. If leadership is not "of the Spirit of God," then what is it? The church of God is a supernatural community, blood-bought and Spirit-filled. Leaders must be spiritual themselves, selected in a way that indicates the Holy Spirit has gifted them to lead.

An Exhorted Leadership

Leaders must not be only instructed, not only appointed, but also exhorted to be faithful to the task. This was actually what Paul was doing right here in the heart of this passage. This was a critical part of Paul's farewell address to these leaders because he was aware that he was leaving them. Paul was commissioning this leadership in a new and special way to take on the role of guarding and guiding the life of the church. "Therefore take heed to yourselves and to all the flock . . . to shepherd the church of God which He purchased with His own blood" (v. 28). That was what they were to do—to take heed, to watch, to be vigilant, to be watchers, to be workers, to shepherd, to lead, to care for, to protect the sheep. What a moment this must have been! What a sense of significance must have permeated the air as Paul was speaking. The apostle, who had already said they were not going to see his face anymore, was commissioning them afresh to this task of shepherding. If this was depicted in a movie scene, I'm sure the cameras would move back and forth between Paul and these leaders listening to him. I'm sure these leaders waited on every word and hardly moved as Paul spoke. It is hard to guess at the actual sound of Paul's voice, but I'm sure his tone was serious and direct. What a moment in time! Praise God that this scene has been given to us in Luke's account of the continued work of Jesus by His Spirit, making disciples and taking the gospel to one of the major cities of the world.

But let's move on in this passage of Scripture. Paul went on to say, "For I know this, that after my departure savage wolves will come in among you, not sparing the flock. Also from among yourselves men will rise up, speaking perverse things, to draw away the disciples after themselves. Therefore watch, and remember that for three years I did not cease to warn everyone night and day with tears" (vv. 29–31). What was Paul saying? He warned them that problems were going to come into the church from outside (v. 29). But he also warned, "From among yourselves men will rise up, speaking perverse things, to draw away the disciples after themselves" (v. 30). In other words, problems were also going to arise from within the church.

Christ is building His church, and the gates of hell will not prevail against it (Matt. 16:18). It is His sovereign plan through His saving work to build His people, His bride, His church. But this does not negate the real problems that are a part of church life and ministry. How practical and prophetic Paul's words were and are. These leaders were getting a reality check from the wise apostle. This was in the apostolic age, with the freshness of the Word of God and the work of the Holy Spirit. And yet Paul didn't say, "Folks, it'll be smooth sailing." He did not say, "You won't have any problems." He didn't say, "Trust God and everything will be okay." No, the role of the leader is to watch, to guard, and to protect. In this case Paul was both warning and preparing them for the problems they were going to experience. These problems would come from the outside by way of persecution, pressure, or false teachers—those "savage wolves" who would come into the church, "not sparing the flock" (Acts 20:29). Paul uses strong language, and so should we as we think about people who would harm God's people spiritually or physically. The leader needs to be aware of people, movements, and practices in the environment of the church that could creep in unnoticed (Jude 4). Ultimately, though, even movements and practices do not come in detached from specific people. These leaders were to be on the lookout for ruthless, destructive people who could damage the life of the church. Paul said, "I know this" (v. 29), meaning that these leaders could expect such dangerous people. They could bank on it.

But problems would also arise from within the church itself. Even under the influence of the Word and the Holy Spirit, under the eyesight of faithful leaders, problems would emerge. To be more accurate, Paul actually said, "Men will rise up" (v. 30). That says something about the sinfulness of people. It says something about the subtly of Satan. It says something about the need for us to be on the alert.

Notice that the emphasis here is on what these people were going to say—"perverse things"—and on their motivation—"to draw away the disciples after themselves" (v. 30). Leaders must be prepared. Leaders don't need to be naïve about how people operate. Leaders should be loving, gracious, caring in every respect, seeking to be Christlike in manner but prepared and realistic about the people and problems that are to be experienced. Furthermore, leaders must know the truth and be able to defend it. Also, leaders need to be able to discern error and refute it—to have eyes, ears, and noses that can sense danger and deal with it.

For example, we read Paul's instructions to Titus to "appoint elders in every city" (Titus 1:5). These elders were to hold fast to "the faithful word" taught, so as to "be able, by sound doctrine, both to exhort and convict those who contradict" (v. 9). Paul then described some of the problematic people in Crete that these leaders were to encounter (vv. 10–16). Paul clearly told Titus that he left him in Crete to "set in order the things that are lacking, and [to] appoint elders in every city as I commanded you" (v. 5). So we see that this matter of protective leadership was of utmost importance.

The problems we face today in church life are not new. We see such problems right from the start in the book of Acts. We also know that people have not changed fundamentally. People from outside the church and people within the church will cause serious problems. Furthermore, we know that in this world, there will always be truth and there will always be error. When we see a church going through a difficult time, we should pray and be available to help if appropriate, but we really shouldn't be surprised. Leaders ought to be prepared to handle the crisis, being watchful over "the flock of God" (1 Pet. 5:2).

An Entrusted Leadership

"So now, brethren, I commend [entrust] you to God and to the word of His grace, which is able to build you up and give you an inheritance among all those who are sanctified" (Acts 20:32). What do I mean by "entrusted leadership"? Paul placed these beloved leaders in God's hands with God's Word to support them and build them up. He would not be able to stand by them daily. He was leaving. He would not see them again. So how were they to carry on their responsibility? How were they going to lead? They were going to lead as God enabled and empowered them on the basis of His Word. Paul in a very special and significant sense was giving these leaders over to God.

This is a very important part of delegation in the leadership process. There is a time when people are instructed, appointed, exhorted, and commissioned. But then these leaders need to be entrusted. They need to be handed over to God, to the instruction they have received, and to the Word that can sustain them. Then they have the full responsibility, God helping them. In other words, Paul said, "You now need to depend on God and His Word alone. The job is in your hands. I'm moving on." That was Paul's pattern.

We live in a day of fast travel and instant communication. Even if founders, mentors, and former leaders are at a distance, they can often still be available by phone or e-mail. So it is hard to sense the finality of Paul's words concerning his departure from these Ephesian leaders in Acts 20. I don't think Paul was saying they would never hear from him again. But he was not going to physically be "there" for them in the future. God would be there for them, though, as would the powerful Word of grace. Therefore, despite the anticipated problems, Paul was not a pessimist. He knew the power of God and the efficacy of God's Word. I believe Paul expected the church at Ephesus to be built up and that the believers would receive an eternal inheritance. These leaders and the church would be in good hands—God's hands.

I want to encourage you right now to take a few moments to think about these questions: What do you want to leave behind? What will be the lasting legacies of your life and your leadership role? You may say, "Well, I'm not really a leader." But you are a person of influence within your circle: your family, your business, your ministry, your church, your community, etc. What do you want to leave behind for them? The reason you need to know this is because your desired legacies will help you set your current priorities and goals. So why not write out on a piece of paper what you would like to leave behind? Better yet, why not write out your own "farewell address," and then live in the light of it?

When the apostle Paul anticipated his heavenly departure as we read in 2 Timothy 4:6—"I am already being poured out as a drink offering, and the time of my departure is at hand"—he could say, "I have fought the good fight, I have finished the race, I have kept the faith. Finally, there is laid up for me the crown of righteousness, which the Lord, the righteous Judge, will give to me on that Day, and not to me only but also to all who have loved His appearing" (vv. 7–8).

These are not arrogant words. These are not self-confident words. These are the words of a man who lived with clear priorities and goals.

Likewise, as Paul addressed the leaders in Ephesus he could say, "You know my personal example. You remember my preached word, and you are my prepared leadership." I trust that the Lord will help us to have this kind of vision and passion that leads to specific legacies of life and service as we seek to be people of influence.

Part Two:
Responsibilities *to* Fulfill

CHAPTER 4

Having a Reason
ROMANS 15:14–33

Even though my father was a very gifted and brilliant man, he was easy to understand. I am not talking about his use of language or vocabulary, although he was a master communicator. I'm talking about his life. He was easy to understand because you knew his motivating reasons and driving passions. You knew he wanted to do God's will with all his heart. You knew he wanted to live a holy life. You knew he wanted to be like Christ. You knew he wanted to live each day with the Holy Spirit filling his life, ungrieved and unquenched. You knew he wanted to preach the Word. You knew he wanted to encourage and equip others who were preaching the Word. These goals were behind the decisions he made. These concerns or motivations helped explain not only what he did but also the way he did what he did.

Frankly, it is easy to follow the leadership of someone whose reasons for decisions and actions are clear and consistent. The difficulty comes when you are not sure of a leader's motivations or rationales. Then decisions and actions can be hard to understand or follow.

Faithful leaders must have good reasons for what they are doing and where they are going. The "reason" or the "why" for what is being done acts like a flowing river, keeping the leaders within the banks of faithfulness to their calling and mission. Furthermore, communicating such reasons and goals helps followers or potential followers understand and trust the leader's purpose and plan.

At various times Paul shared his own perspective and approach to ministry. I want us to look at one of the apostle's explanations that is tied directly to specific plans and practical decisions. Romans 15:14–33 will give us insights into how ministry vision and mission were tied to ministry decisions in his life.

In the previous section, we saw Paul giving a "farewell address" at the conclusion of a phase of ministry. The Roman epistle gives us insights into Paul's thinking as he anticipates a future phase of ministry. In this passage Paul introduces himself and his gospel in the light of his plans to go to Rome, to preach there, and to be sent on to Spain.

If we were to try reducing Paul's explanations in these verses to one central concept, it is this: *he was exercising a God-given ministry according to God's calling.* It was on the basis of this ministry (and different aspects of it) that he did everything. It was due to this "grace" to be a "minister of Jesus Christ to the Gentiles" (Rom. 15:15–16) that he wrote this Roman epistle "more boldly ... on some points" (v. 15). I'm not sure which points Paul was referring to, but the rationale for his bold manner in writing was due to his God-given ministry and authority.

In verse 22 we read, "For this reason I also have been much hindered from coming to you." What reason? The God-given ministry he was exercising. That's what had kept him from coming to Rome in the past (1:13) despite often planning to do so. His absence had not been due to a lack of desire or planning. Rather, his decision not to go to Rome had been based on the ministry he was doing at the time. Since he had now finished a geographical phase of his work, he was finally planning to come to Rome (15:23–24).

Still, as a testimony to the continuance of his God-given ministry, his itinerary included more than just Rome. After spending some time there, he desired to be sent on his way to Spain. Why? Because this was in keeping with the ministry he explained in verses 16–21.

Even so, Paul was not on his way to Rome at that very moment! He explained in the next verses that before he would be free to travel to Rome, he first needed to go to Jerusalem (vv. 25–28). Why? Paul was delivering funds for the poor "saints" in Jerusalem, which represented the conclusion of his present phase of ministry. This collection project, which is explained in some detail (vv. 26–28), was a significant part of his God-given ministry to the Gentiles. It would not be until these funds were delivered and Paul "sealed to them this fruit" (v. 28) that he would be free to travel to Rome and Spain. In light of this immediate ministry and his subsequent travel plans, he requested fervent prayer.

You may be thinking, "Why all of these details about Paul's writing style, past ministry, immediate travel plans, future travel plans, and so forth?" It's because I want you to see what tied together all these decisions, plans, and activities. Paul had a reason for what he *had been* doing, what he *was* doing, and what he *intended* to do. It all came back to his God-given ministry. Yes, at first glance, one could be confused: Paul talks about not being able to come to Rome, but now able to come to Rome, not coming directly to Rome, not staying indefinitely in Rome, traveling on to Spain, going first to Jerusalem, and writing this bold letter "on some points." But such matters are the "stuff" of life, are they not? We often seem to be moving in different directions at the same time. But leaders need to ask if there is some reason behind it all that makes sense. Is there a consistent motivation that can be seen as the details of our lives, our service, and our mission are viewed? Despite the complicated movements of the apostle, we can see that they all point back to the God-given ministry he was exercising.

Take a look at how Paul described this God-given ministry. Certainly Paul's apostolic ministry was unique, but I believe there are lessons to be learned by viewing Paul's explanation of his ministry in this context.

GOD-GIVEN POSITION

Paul stated clearly that he served in a God-given position "because of the grace given to me by God, that I might be a minister of Jesus Christ to the Gentiles, ministering the gospel of God, that the offering of the Gentiles might be acceptable, sanctified by the Holy Spirit" (vv. 15–16). Here Paul describes his ministry role in priestly and sacrificial terms. He also describes his ministry in Trinitarian terms. Both of these observations point to a God-centered approach to ministry.

Paul's ministry *started* with God and *ended* with God. The key word indicating the "God-given-ness" of the ministry is "grace" (Rom. 1:5; 12:3; 15:15). This grace seems to include the ideas of calling, gifting, enabling, and authorizing. This was a "received" ministry from God. But it also was a ministry that was God-directed. The fruit of the ministry was to be an offering back to God. Paul used sacrificial language here to portray what the apostolic preaching of the gospel to the Gentiles was all about.

There are various interpretations and implications of these words that could receive attention here,[1] but I want us to see one main truth in Paul's language. Paul's position and ministry were not part of a man-made and man-centered enterprise. Paul was on a mission *from* God, *to* God, and *through* God. Graced by God and as a minister of Christ, the gospel was to be proclaimed in order that the Gentiles might believe on Christ for salvation (Rom. 1:16; 10:9–10). Sanctified by the Holy Spirit, they were now to offer their lives to God. Paul had a God-given position that resulted in a God-centered approach to ministry.

This God-centered understanding of Paul's position and ministry needs to challenge us. In ministry and in leadership specifically, God must be our beginning and our end. God must give us what we are to do, and we must offer it back to Him. Such a conviction is not a cause for arrogance or boasting in our role or ability. Rather, we recognize that we are totally dependent upon God and accountable to Him.

God-given Power

It is interesting that Paul explained next his "reason to glory" (15:17) as he sought to summarize what had been taking place in his ministry. But he was careful to glory "in Christ Jesus in the things which pertain to God" (v. 17). He said, "I will not dare to speak of any of those things which Christ has not accomplished through me, in word and deed, to make the Gentiles obedient—in mighty signs and wonders, by the power of the Spirit of God" (vv. 18–19).

Central to all of this "glorying" is what I call the *God-given power* that accomplished the ministry. Christ did it all through him! The means Christ used were words and deeds, but Christ was the One who did it, not Paul! To what end or purpose was this activity? It was "to make the Gentiles obedient." The goal was the fruit, not just of a collection (v. 28), but the fruit of lives now offered to God in Christ.

Paul drew attention to the accompanying miracles and evidences of God-given power, things accomplished "by the power of the Spirit of God" (v. 19). Notice that the goal was not that these "mighty signs and wonders" took place (v. 19). The goal was the obedience of the Gentiles, which speaks of their response to the gospel (12:1–2). But the central truth for us to emphasize here is that this goal was accomplished by Christ and by the power of the Holy Spirit.

Praise God for every authentic manifestation of His power as we seek to lead and minister for His purpose and glory. We will come back to this matter of purpose or goal in a moment, but we must always remember that it is God's power that accomplishes what needs to be accomplished. It is easy to pay lip service to this, but we often think and act otherwise. We can stress the human agency, process, program, or institution that "made" it all happen. We give God the glory, but not really.

God-given power is the key dynamic to authentic leadership and ministry. Without Christ working through us, our work is not fully His! Oh, I understand that God sovereignly orchestrates the works of man for His purposes, and He grants authority as He wills. Jesus told Pilate, when Pilate sought to impress the suffering Savior with his political power, "You could have no power at all against Me unless it had been given you from above" (John 19:11). God places people where He wills, and their power is only as He allows. But in the context of Romans 15, we can go further and deeper. We are talking here about Christian leadership and ministry that is intentionally seeking to be used of God, depending upon God's power to bring about God-glorifying purposes.

In another context Paul speaks of his "striving" in ministry "according to His working which works in me mightily" (Col. 1:29). Paul's power source was God Himself—God's power working in him and through him. Such power did not just manifest itself in outward miracles but in the necessary grace to handle "infirmities" (2 Cor. 12:1–10). But such power enabled ministry to take place. Paul knew this and "boasted" in Christ Jesus accordingly.

GOD-GIVEN PURPOSE

This God-given position infused with God-given power was to achieve a God-given purpose or goal. We have already pointed out that the purpose or goal was the obedience of the Gentiles. But how was Paul to go about doing this? What was his strategy for doing what God called him to do? Well, Paul goes on to say, "So that from Jerusalem and round about to Illyricum I have fully preached the gospel of Christ. And so I have made it my aim to preach the gospel, not where Christ was named, lest I should build on another man's foundation, but as it is written: 'To whom He was not announced, they shall see; and those who have not heard shall understand'" (Rom. 15:19–21).

Paul's understanding of his calling was informed by the Scriptures. This became the basis for his priority and strategy in ministry to achieve his God-given purpose. Paul's aim was to preach the gospel. This aim was at the heart of the "grace" and apostleship he received to be used of God to bring about "obedience to the faith among all nations for His Name" (1:5). This preaching ministry, of course, did not simply mean to declare gospel truths but to do the necessary activities that surrounded such a preaching ministry. These are reflected in Acts, as we have seen, and are spelled out further in Paul's epistles. But the preaching of the gospel was Paul's aim. Due to his calling to the nations (Gentiles), this demanded a missiological and geographical strategy. The motivation behind this strategy was to "fully preach the gospel of Christ" (15:19). This seems to indicate a desire on his part to see the gospel preached fully in a given area, which Paul states as being "from Jerusalem and round about to Illyricum" (v. 19). It was finishing this task of preaching the gospel fully within this area that had kept Paul from turning his attention to Rome and beyond.

The fact that Paul started with Jerusalem, even though we know he was set apart at Antioch, indicates that Paul had a fuller and deeper perspective on the gospel ministry. He was concerned for areas that he had not personally evangelized. But more than that, he recognized Jerusalem as the starting place for mission. Indeed, he was returning there as he wrote this epistle to demonstrate the fruit of the Gentile mission as they contributed to the needs in Jerusalem. How much we read into the word "Jerusalem" here is a question, but such a geographical understanding of his mission is certainly in keeping with his declaration in Romans 1:16, "for the Jew first and also for the Greek."

Why Paul ends with Illyricum must be based on the facts of his mission. But just to speculate for a moment: Illyricum must have been viewed as the outer region of the area he had covered so far. He certainly had a sense of satisfaction that the foundational work he was performing had been accomplished. Evidently, what work remained to be done was not his responsibility. Now he was free to set his sights on Rome and beyond.

The book of Acts is needed to give us Paul's movements during his missionary journeys. We see a basic strategy driven by this need to preach in new areas where the gospel had not been preached (Rom. 15:20). As the apostle to the nations, Paul was not seeking to build upon others' ministries; rather he was seeking to pioneer the gospel into untouched areas. Within this basic strategy, we also see movements impacted by the reception given to the gospel, the leading of the Spirit of God, persecution, and circumstances. So within the framework of the mission, there were various movements and activities as the ministry proceeded and developed. But looking back on it all, the apostle saw a completed work according to what God had called him to do.

The relevant comment for us to note is that Paul's strategy was based upon his priority or purpose, not the other way around. The aim or goal was clear. The strategy did not wag the purpose; rather, the purpose drove the strategy (as it should). And the purpose was God-given, no question about it! This is exemplary for us in ministry and leadership as we try to develop particular strategies, processes, and programs. We cannot lose sight of the God-given purpose, whatever it is, as we proceed.

Paul's understanding of his mission was viewed biblically as well. In Romans 15:21, for example, he quoted Isaiah 52:15 to lend support and understanding to his readers concerning the nature of his ministry. Romans is simply filled with Old Testament quotations, including the one that undergirds Paul's presentation of the gospel: "The just shall live by faith" (Hab. 2:4, in Rom. 1:17). There is a sense in which the Habakkuk quotation gives support for what Paul was preaching. In Romans 15:21, Paul was giving scriptural support for what he was doing: "To whom He was not announced, they shall see; and those who have not heard shall understand." Paul was on solid ground in terms of his mission. His ministry was *of* God, *by* God, *for* God, and *with* God. What he was doing was based on the Word of God as well as the direct calling he had received.

Without stretching the application too far, it is safe to say that we as leaders and Christian workers should have a biblical/theological reason for what we are doing in ministry. We may have sensed the call of God in any number of ways, but it is always important to align our sense of call with a specific biblical principle and pattern. Even though Paul only quoted one verse as he spoke of his foundational ministry, his use of Scripture elsewhere makes it clear that he saw himself within God's redemptive plan and mission. Paul was not acting outside of the will of God; rather, he was involved in the great enterprise of reaching the nations with the gospel of Christ. We need to have a conviction based on the Word of God that what we are doing is of God, is empowered by God, and that the purpose and accompanying strategy are pleasing to God.

Faithful leaders and people in ministry need a good reason for what they are doing. This includes being in a God-given position, relying on God-given power, seeking to achieve a God-given purpose. Such are the characteristics of a faithful leader. And a faithful leader should have an approach to ministry that is God-centered in these significant ways. How we need faithful leaders and authentic ministry!

So What?

You may be thinking, "This sounds good, but what practical difference does all this make for me in my situation?" Well, I actually don't know your situation, but let me try to answer the question anyway. We all need to be faithful to God's calling, God's leading, and God's plan for our lives. To begin with, God must be at the center of our thinking, planning, and doing. We must have a God-shaped rationale for what we are doing and how we are doing it. In a similar fashion to the apostle Paul, we need a passion to follow and complete God's plan. And this passion and commitment will impact all of life, including our daily decisions. So we need to evaluate, first of all, whether or not we are living God-centered lives. Is our passion the glory of God in every area of life? Then we need to discern God's calling and priorities for us. As best as we can discern, what has God given us to do? What is God's mission for us specifically? And what do we need to be doing right now as a part of this mission? Assuming that we have a sense of what God wants us to do, and we have a commitment to do it, how do we get it done?

I want to answer this question in a way that is true to Scripture, relevant for all Christians, and especially important for leaders. First of all, there is the important matter of *God-directed confidence*. When a person knows they are doing something in the will of God and for God's glory, they can have confidence in God's enabling and pleasure. Confidence then is not placed in self, in others, in circumstances, or whatever. Confidence can be placed in God alone, in whom it belongs! You sense this God-directed confidence in the apostle Paul's words in Romans 15:29, "But I know that when I come to you, I shall come in the fullness of the blessing of the gospel of Christ." What a statement! And this statement needs to be viewed in the light of all that we have said in the previous verses. Paul's confidence was in the Lord, and he had such confidence not only because he knew the Lord but because he knew he was involved in God-given ministry. He sensed that when he completed the task at hand, which was critical to his current ministry plan, he would be able to come with God's blessing. Such confidence in God is crucial for good and faithful leadership. Without it, the leader is "sunk" spiritually—and will not *enjoy* ministry either.

Alongside of God-directed confidence is *God-directed dependence.* Paul ends this section of his epistle with a plea for prayer (vv. 30–33). This plea that mentions "the Lord Jesus Christ," "the Spirit," and "God," is a passionate plea for fervent prayers for protection and deliverance, acceptable service in Jerusalem, and safe travel to Rome. You might question, Well, if Paul has such confidence in God, why is he asking for prayer? He is asking for prayer *because* he has confidence in God!

Confidence in God means that we must depend upon Him. Confidence in God does not erase the realities we face or the challenges we confront. But such realities must be faced with dependence upon the God we trust. So Paul invites these Roman believers into the fellowship of prayer with him in order to seek God's activity in the ways expressed. The leader must depend upon God. He is our source and resource. We bring others into the circle of dependence, but together we must look to the Lord for help. Lack of prayer may indicate lack of confidence in God, lack of dependence upon Him, or a lack of understanding concerning the problems and issues we face. Paul knew exactly what the dangers were in returning to Jerusalem. This was not just an off-the-cuff "pray for me."

I am reminded of a wonderful time of fellowship I was privileged to have with a man named Romulo Saune. He came through Memphis many years ago, and we talked together about his amazing ministry in Peru. He was a man of humility and compassion, one who had a great burden for his people. He served in a very dangerous context to which he was scheduled to return. He shared with me the dangers that surrounded him, the believers, and the ministry that was taking place. And yet he made a definite decision to return to his homeland for the sake of Christ, the people, and the ministry. I received the news a few weeks after his departure that he had been shot and killed in an ambush back in Peru. His confidence was in the Lord, the One on whom he depended. This enabled him to go back to this place of danger and even to die in the line of duty for his Master. He is a hero in my book, a man faithful to the Lord and God's will until the sudden end of his life.

The apostle Paul faced serious danger in returning to Jerusalem. We know from the book of Acts that Paul was arrested in the temple and was near death on numerous occasions before he finally reached Rome. His confidence and dependence were in the Lord, and yet he knew the real dangers ahead.

Ministry includes real challenges and dangers. If our reason is not solid, our confidence can waver and our dependence can shift to other people or things. These are essential tools for the leader. Without confidence in and dependence upon the Lord, it is hard to lead faithfully.

I vaguely remember an incident we faced in our own family when my father was the pastor of Calvary Baptist Church in New York City. To cut a long story short, a very angry man killed two policemen and said he was coming for my father. In the end, the man killed himself and the whole crisis was over. Such things happen in ministry because you are dealing with people—with *sinful* people. The servant of the Lord has to depend upon the Lord, and confidence needs to be placed in the Lord alone.

The last part of my answer to the "So what?" question has to do with determination or perseverance. These words are not used in our text, but they are qualities evident in the life of Paul and sensed throughout his explanation of his ministry in Romans 15:14–33. Paul had persevered through much ministry already, a very tough assignment was right in front of him, and he still had a big vision for the future. Paul was a man of determination, a *God-enabled determination*. Paul passionately wanted to finish his God-given work. He wanted to see it through to the end. That's what leaders do. Faithful leaders are those who see things through to the end with determination. The end may mean different things, but the desire and determination to complete the mission should be there

One is likely to think of Nehemiah in this regard. (We'll look more closely at the example of Nehemiah in chapter 8.) When he heard of the current conditions in Jerusalem—the distress and reproach—he wept, fasted, and prayed (Neh. 1:1–11). He prayed specifically for an opportunity to respond to the situation. Then he *took* the opportunity when the king spoke to him. Under "the good hand of my God," and supplied by the king, Nehemiah went to Jerusalem (2:1–10, esp. v. 8). He viewed the walls there and organized the rebuilding plan (2:11–3:32). He defended the wall and the workers (4:1–23), dealt with problems and issues (5:1–18), and resisted direct opposition to the project (6:1–14). The initial task that he undertook—the rebuilding of the walls—was accomplished in fifty-two days (6:15–16). Nehemiah would do much more, but this overview reveals a man determined to see a job done. His determination was to serve in a God-given purpose, which put him in a God-given position while relying upon God-given power. Nehemiah was a man of confidence and dependence upon God, which solidly undergirded his determination to see through to the end the task God had given. It all started with a "good reason"—a God-shaped reason.

What Now?

It may be helpful for you to express in writing the reason you are doing what you are doing right now in the Lord's service. As a leader, what is the reason (or reasons) behind it all? If you have some big decisions to make concerning your leadership or ministry, make sure these decisions are in tune with these valid reasons. Will your decision be faithful to your God-given ministry and/or position? Will your decision lead you into the assurance of God-given power? Will this decision further a God-given purpose that needs to be accomplished?

To be a faithful leader, one has to be in touch with the "why" behind what is taking place. This is a constant matter for prayer, reaffirmation, and communication. May we be faithful to the Lord and His cause. May we be faithful to His calling and complete what He has given us to do.

CHAPTER 5
Guarding the Heart
1 KINGS 11:1–13

At the heart of the matter of faithfulness is the heart of God's servant. And one of the primary ways the heart of God's servant is revealed is by how the heart of God's servant responds to God's Word. We need to take a serious look at this issue, since it is critical for Christian leaders and people of influence to have hearts "given" to the Lord. One of the primary ways to assess the condition of our spiritual hearts is to allow our hearts to be inspected by the Word of God itself. In other words, we need to allow the Word of God to expose any sin or spiritual problem that needs to be addressed. Then we must respond to this exposure of any sin or wrong by "getting right" through confession, repentance, and a fresh commitment to heartfelt obedience and righteousness. This is a very important aspect of our walk with God and our regular devotional life. Certainly there are other key aspects of our relationship with the Lord, but dealing with sin and avoiding spiritual decline and disaster are fundamental as we seek to live and serve as fallen and redeemed people in a fallen, sin-sick world.

The message of this chapter is summed up by the directive found in Proverbs 4:23: "Keep your heart with all diligence, for out of it spring the issues of life." Sadly, indeed tragically, many people do not finish the Christian race well. Christians who once passionately followed the Lord leave their first love (Rev. 2:4) and find themselves in need of repentance, the rebuke of the Lord, and restoration.

But let me speak personally: my concern is for my own heart. I want to stay true to the Lord. I want a heart after God. I want to be faithful to the Lord. I want to be a Caleb who was the same at eighty-five as he was at forty. The Scripture says of Caleb, "He wholly followed the LORD God of Israel" (Josh. 14:14). What a testimony! It was true of him at the age of forty (v. 8) and again at eighty-five. Such faithfulness and consistency indicate a heart yielded to God and committed to obedience.

There is a work that God must do in our hearts, and we must look to God for that initially and constantly. At the same time, God's servant has a responsibility concerning matters of the heart. It is this responsibility we want to consider by way of two examples. Both of these examples are Old Testament kings, one found in 1 Kings and the other in 2 Kings. Both are key individuals in the history of the Old Testament and both had leadership responsibilities. We start with a tragic example, then we will move to a uniquely positive example to complete the picture.

My goal in giving these examples is to present some basic principles concerning matters of the heart, painting the big picture of this whole issue. For it is ultimately up to each individual to discern his or her own idols, lusts, loves, and areas of weakness that could cause "shipwreck" of their lives, their leadership, and their ministries.

Spiritual Heart Trouble

First of all, let's consider a leader who experienced spiritual heart trouble. And in so doing we will be warned by the tragedy of Solomon's unguarded heart.

The first ten chapters of 1 Kings present one of the most glorious times in the history of Israel. And at the center of these days of strength, prosperity, and expansion is the reign of King Solomon (970s BC to around 930 BC). Solomon was anointed king as his father David desired. He consolidated the throne and dealt with opposition firmly. He was granted wisdom from God in a special encounter (1 Kings 3:5–14), and was shown to be a wise administrator who built the temple and other buildings, including his own house. The dedication of the temple was certainly one of the major events in this period of Israel's history.

This was a time of military victory, expansion, and increasing prosperity. In the midst of this, God met with Solomon a second time and promised the future of the throne and covenantal blessings if he would walk before God "in integrity of heart and in uprightness, to do according to all that I have commanded you" (9:4). If Solomon or his sons were to turn from following the Lord, the consequences would be serious and severe (vv. 1–9). So he knew the requirements of faithfulness, and he knew the consequences of both faithfulness and unfaithfulness.

Chapter 10 of 1 Kings is a description of King Solomon's wisdom and wealth. Putting together the first ten chapters gives you a picture of a man who had it all—heritage, authority, wisdom, accomplishments, power, wealth, respect, praise, and spiritual blessings. But chapter 11 reveals a problem that can best be described as spiritual heart trouble or spiritual heart disease, which shows itself with the following causes and symptoms:

A MISPLACED LOVE

Solomon loved what he should not have loved and wanted what he did not need. God had commanded that the Israelites should not marry foreign women because they served other gods and would turn their hearts away. It is clear from the text that Solomon "loved" many foreign women (1 Kings 11:1); he "clung to these in love" (v. 2). This was not the case of a brief fling on Solomon's part. He had a continuous love and involvement outside of the will of God. He had a misplaced love. When we love and go after something outside of God's revealed will for us, there will be trouble. But at the deepest level, such a pursuit and practice reveals a heart that is not in harmony with the Lord.

DISOBEDIENT ACTS

Ultimately, Solomon's sin was disobeying the direct command of God as expressed in verse 2: "You shall not intermarry with them, nor they with you. Surely they will turn away your hearts after their gods." Whether Solomon's motive was personal or political, he still disobeyed a clear command of Scripture. According to Deuteronomy 17:17, a king was not to "multiply wives for himself," and the count in 1 Kings 11:3 reveals that Solomon went overboard in this matter as well. He multiplied to himself many wives and concubines who did not worship the Lord. Solomon's disobedience exposed his heart trouble. But not only so, it also brought about the turning of his heart away from total and unrivaled devotion to the Lord.

UNGODLY INFLUENCES

God had warned that such disobedience would result in the turning away of the heart from God. The influence of these ungodly alliances would be serious and debilitating. These marriages would result in a spiritual turning away from the Lord. And according to the Scriptures, that is exactly what happened.

Let's just stop for a moment and think: if you are reading these last few paragraphs with a sense of the context of 1 Kings, you might be thinking or asking, "How in the world could this happen to Solomon? I thought he knew the Lord. I thought he had everything a man could want. And even more, I thought he was the wisest man around!" Yes, he knew the Lord. Yes, he had just about everything. Yes, he had God-given wisdom. But, but, but . . .

There is something about the human heart that defies simple explanation, for the heart is deceitful and desperately wicked (Jer. 17:9). James affirms that the real problem behind outward conflicts comes from the passions and lust within (James 4:1–3). So we have to be careful about matters of the heart. And in this regard as well as in all matters of temptation, we need to hear and heed the words of the apostle Paul: "Therefore let him who thinks he stands take heed lest he fall" (1 Cor. 10:12).

If it could happen to Solomon, then we need to guard our hearts from loves, passions, and lusts that are not of God, are not His will for us, and are not pleasing to Him. The wisest man in all the world had an area of his life that was out of the will of God and frankly out of control. Solomon had so much to lose through such disobedience, but somehow the promised consequences did not deter him from what he wanted at a very deep level.

It is good to ask ourselves honestly, "What do we really want?" What are our real desires and passions? Is there some out-of-control aspect of our lives that reveals something is wrong with our hearts? Leaders must especially ask themselves these questions because the consequences of an unguarded heart will impact the decisions we make, the actions we take, and the people we serve.

A Divided Heart

As Solomon grew older, his heart became weakened and he demonstrated a divided heart. The man who built the temple was tolerating and promoting idolatry in Israel. "Say it ain't so! How could this be?"

The reality of what is taking place in our text should strike us. Think about all that went into the building of the temple and what it symbolized for the people of God. Think about the ongoing temple practices, services, and celebrations that surely continued. Solomon had a divided heart in contrast to his father, David (1 Kings 11:4). David certainly had his own sins and problems (to say the least), but here Solomon is contrasted negatively with David. As we will note again later, David had a heart for God and knew what repentance was—despite his sins. We don't see this sensitivity on Solomon's part. His heart was divided and disloyal to the Lord.

A Disobedient Lifestyle

There is no evidence in the text that Solomon changed his pattern of behavior. He developed a lifestyle of disobedience. He tolerated and participated in idolatry. He built high places and allowed false worship in the nation. The text says that "he did likewise for all his foreign wives" (v. 8), meaning that Solomon continued in this condition. How sad a picture! It all seems so ridiculous, even if one allows for the culture of the day and the pressures of power and leadership. The Scriptures do not emphasize any of the factors that could make us feel sorry for Solomon or better understand his circumstances. We are just told that he did what God had said not to do, and this became a pattern in his life—the wisest man in all the world!

It is easy to look at cultural pressures and personal circumstances when seeking a rationale for disobedience. But we must look directly to the Lord and His Word with an undivided heart to discern and determine how we are to live. And within the broader scope of obedient living, we need to seek the Lord's will in the specific area of life that is addressed by the Word of God.

The High Cost of Spiritual Heart Trouble

Solomon was not above God's covenant or law. God responded to his sin and heart trouble. God had already spelled out the potential disaster if Solomon or his sons were to disobey the Lord and "turn from following [Him]" (1 Kings 9:6). But we learn in 1 Kings 11:9–13 that Solomon was made aware, in no uncertain terms, of the consequences of his disobedience.

FACING GOD'S PERSONAL ANGER

God is a personal God, and although He loves us, He will discipline us. There are consequences to what we do. It may be hard for us to grasp the righteous anger of God, since we have so few good human models. But we must always remember that God is a Person, and He has loves and hates. In New Testament language, it is possible to grieve the Holy Spirit (Eph. 4:30) by what we do. It is possible to quench the Holy Spirit (1 Thess. 5:19). In short, God can be displeased and righteously angry at sinful behavior.

What is sad is that Solomon had been experiencing so much of God's favor and blessing, and now "his heart had turned from the LORD" (1 Kings 11:9). This turning of the heart is associated directly with the king's disobedience and his failure to keep God's covenant and statutes.

As a leader Solomon was not above the Law, so to speak. Indeed he should have been the one *leading* Israel in covenantal faithfulness and obedience.

Receiving God's Penetrating Words

God told Solomon that He was going to tear away the kingdom. Everything he had worked for and dreamed about was going to be lost, not in *his* day, but in his *son's* day. The loss would be personal, familial, and national. These words from the Lord must have devastated Solomon. A servant would get the kingdom rather than his own son. Twice the name of David is mentioned, and once Jerusalem is mentioned as God explains His actions. Out of covenant loyalty to David and His faithfulness to His chosen city, the tearing of the kingdom would not happen in Solomon's day, and Solomon's son would end up with one tribe.

The contrast between Solomon and David is important to note again. This is one of the ways that the emphasis of the text is reinforced. Six times the word "heart" appears in the English text, and it was exactly the "heart" issue that separated Solomon from his father David.

Experiencing God's Sovereign Actions

"The LORD raised up an adversary against Solomon" (1 Kings 11:14). How tragic! After all the years of blessing, God now began to work out His plan of judgment according to His words. In the rest of this chapter and the remainder of 1 and 2 Kings, we see that God did exactly what He said. As you read 1 and 2 Kings, you follow the sad story of moving from "glory" to "exile." The early chapters of 1 Kings tell us of the glory days of Solomon's reign. But a downward spiral begins in 1 Kings 11:14, ending with the king of Judah in Babylon (2 Kings 25:27–30). There is evidence of God's continued mercy, but God's people are scattered, in exile, and in need of restoration.

The leader needs to know that he is doing God's will and that he is in the flow of God's plan and power. It is tragic when a leader finds himself outside the will of God and in some way experiencing less than

God's blessing. God continues to be at work in our world for His purpose and glory. One should not be premature in making judgments about the presence or absence of the authentic work of God. But it certainly can be the case that one can be in a position of leadership without experiencing God's power. Indeed, God has a way of disciplining His servants today, even if it is not as obvious or drastic as what happened to the children of Israel in 1 and 2 Kings. From what I can see, this text is a turning point in the history of Israel. Before 1 Kings 11, there is every sign of covenantal blessing and abundance. After 1 Kings 11:13, we learn of the adversarial role of God and the beginnings of the divided kingdom. The account ends with both Israel and Judah found in exile, removed from the land of promise. This is serious business!

Preventive Care for Spiritual Heart Trouble

Before we move to our positive example, what can we glean from this negative example? In short, I take this account to be a warning text in the Scriptures. The text warns us to guard our hearts. But how? Are there any practical instructions or implications we can glean from this text? I believe that preventive measures can be gleaned for the person who does not want to end up in exile in terms of the purpose and blessing of God. Let's briefly consider a number of implications for Christians and Christian leaders especially:

Healthy Fear of the Consequences of Sin

We know there is forgiveness of sins, and we praise God for His mercy, grace, and provision in Christ. There is 1 John 1:7–9 in the Bible, and there is a way back to right fellowship with God (James 4:7–10). The Lord may meet us by the sea, as He did Peter. He may seek to ignite our love afresh for Him and call us back into service, even after behavior that denies Him (see John 21:15–23).

Having said this, we should have a healthy fear of the consequences of sin. We should passionately desire to please the Lord and not miss being in the center of His will. Consequences can be experienced in numerous ways, even if sins are forgiven. This text reveals the very heavy cost of an unguarded heart. And these consequences went way beyond Solomon personally. How tragic! Obviously, we should have a higher level of motivation than avoiding bad consequences, but sometimes when a person is trapped in sin, such a reminder can be greatly used of God to get through a thick head and a diseased heart. There is still a place for warning and admonition in the Christian life. Sadly, such warnings need to be sounded more than they are in the light of frivolous attitudes concerning sin in our own day.

SINCERE REPENTANCE OF ALL KNOWN SIN

Notice the difference between David and Solomon. Four times the name of David appears in our text, so I think it is valid to learn from David's life in contrast to Solomon's life. First Kings 11:6 reads, "Solomon did evil in the sight of the LORD, and did not fully follow the LORD, as did his father David." One has to remember that David was not perfect—far from it! But he had a heart after God. This was manifested in that he was convicted of sin and repented. He suffered the consequences of sin as well, but he seemed to get his heart right with God. David did not follow after other gods. He stayed true to the God of Israel. When sin was exposed, he repented. Solomon did not repent, as far as we can tell from our text. He kept disobeying God with each new foreign wife, and idolatry was multiplied in Israel. A reading of Psalms 32 and 51 would be a good exercise right now. They reflect the heart of someone who wants to be right with God, indeed one who longs for forgiveness, cleansing, and restoration.

PERSONAL COMMITMENT TO FOLLOW THE LORD

This is the contrast between David and Solomon. Such wholehearted following of the Lord is a sign of integrity of heart. Such a commitment will mean guarding our hearts against anything that would cause us to disobey the Lord and develop a pattern of destructive sinful behavior. If the wisest man in the world could be such a bad example, we need to take this matter seriously! We must guard our hearts.

Such a guarding of the heart starts with a loving commitment to obedience. Sinful attitudes and practices must be utterly confessed and renounced. Where obedience has been delayed or neglected, a new pattern of obedience needs to begin. There needs to be a resolve in the power of the Holy Spirit to fully follow the Lord.

Now we turn our attention to someone whose heart turned toward the Lord in contrast to what happened to King Solomon.

A Heart Turns toward the Lord

The text before us is 2 Kings 22:1–23:25. The king is Josiah, and his good example is presented and summarized as follows: "Josiah was eight years old when he became king, and he reigned thirty-one years in Jerusalem. His mother's name was Jedidah the daughter of Adaiah of Bozkath. And he did what was right in the sight of the LORD and walked in all the ways of his father David; he did not turn aside to the right hand or to the left" (22:1–2). "Now before him there was no king like him, who turned to the LORD with all his heart, with all his soul, and with all his might, according to all the Law of Moses; nor after him did any arise like him" (23:25).

The reign of Josiah is described in simple but unprecedented terms: no king before him or after him turned to the Lord in such a complete manner. In light of such a statement in God's Word, it is worth taking a careful look at what is recorded concerning this special king.

Josiah lived and reigned in dark and desperate days, just before the demise of Judah, its defeat, and eventual exile in Babylon. Evil kings had reigned before Josiah, and there was the need for much reform in Judah. Josiah did what was right, bringing about major reforms during his lifetime and reign (640–609 BC).[1] Indeed he brought about a "cleansing" of the nation. We can learn from the record of this godly life and reign.

We can learn what it means to turn to the Lord completely on the basis of His Word. This is a matter of the heart.

A FRESH HEARING OF THE WORD OF GOD

You may remember the story of the high priest Hilkiah finding "the Book of the Law in the house of the LORD" (22:8). Why it had to be found, we do not know! But the seemingly accidental finding of the book of the Law in the house of God led to everything else that happened. Hilkiah gave the book to Shaphan, the scribe. Shaphan read the book, and then he brought the book to the king. He showed the book to the king and then read it before the king. And it was "when the king heard the words of the Book of the Law" that he responded immediately in dramatic fashion: "He tore his clothes" (v. 11).

So often, true personal spiritual change begins with a fresh hearing of the Word of God. This is true on the individual level as well as in great spiritual movements such as the Reformation. When the Word of God is truly heard by people with responsive hearts, spiritual change, movement, and progress take place.

The king "heard the words," in a way that truly impacted his life. We will examine his response more fully in a moment. But first of all, we must ask ourselves if we really believe in the importance of the reading and hearing the Word of God in our day. There is no mention of any explanation or commentary on the part of Shaphan. The response of the king was in light of the simple reading of the Scripture itself. He would also pursue greater understanding, as we will see, but his immediate reaction was to the Word being read.

We need to make sure that the reading of the Word of God is practiced and honored in our private lives. Then we need to read the Word in the context of our families. We should make sure that the Word of God and the reading of it are central in the life of our local churches. Yes, we need to have "ears to hear" what God is saying to us through His Word. There must be a readiness and an openness to God's Word. But such an attitude to the Word is demonstrated in a desire for the Word itself.

My grandfather, Frederick Ernest Samuel Olford, served the Lord for many years as a missionary in what is now Angola. If I were to take you today to where my grandfather is buried in Cardiff, Wales, you would read a simple text on his gravestone, "HIS DELIGHT—THE LAW OF THE LORD" (from Ps. 1:2). It is no surprise that he was greatly used of God in spreading the gospel, planting churches, and teaching the Word of God in Angola. He was part of a translation team that translated the New Testament into the Chokwe language. His ministry was based fully and completely on the Word of God. But this was not just a posture he assumed. He loved the Lord and delighted in His Word. And this delight in the Word of God impacted the way he lived, the way he raised his family, and the way he did ministry.

One of the important practices that defined my father's life and ministry was the regular reading of the Word of God. After my father's death, we found several devotional books he had written in his early twenties. These books were his comments related to his regular reading of the Scriptures. This practice strengthened his spiritual life and laid the foundation for future ministry. We need to read and hear the Word of God.

A Sincere Responding to the Word of God

Josiah models for us someone who responded sincerely to the Word of God in both a personal and public manner. What a contrast to Solomon, a king who apparently ignored the direct command of God and whose disobedience eventually went public!

Notice that Josiah's response was deeply personal (2 Kings 22:11–20). His response could be summarized in two phrases: *he humbled himself*, and *he sought the Lord*. His initial response was to tear his clothes when he heard of the fathers' disobedience to the words of God's Book (v. 13) and God's wrath against "this place and . . . its inhabitants" (v. 19). The tearing of clothes indicated sincere remorse over what he heard. We learn later that the king's "heart was tender," he humbled himself before the Lord, and along with tearing his clothes, he wept (v. 19). The preacher might say in alliterative style that Josiah had torn clothes, tearful eyes, and a tender heart! What a beautiful description of a deeply personal response to God's Word. In short, the king humbled himself. How important to have a receptive and responsive heart to God and His Word.

But the king went further than responding humbly. He sought the Lord. And by seeking the Lord, I mean that he sought to understand more fully what God was saying in His Word and what needed to be done about it. This involved inquiring of the Lord and finding out what God was saying through the prophetess Huldah (vv. 12–20). Our method of inquiry may differ today, but it is important to note the desire of the king to find out what God was really saying to him and for His people at that time. The king sought understanding and the application of God's Word for his own day.

Sadly, the king learned of coming calamity and the outworking of God's wrath because of the people's sin of forsaking God and burning incense to other gods (v. 17). But because of the king's sincere response to the Word of God and the fact that he humbled himself, he would be spared from having to experience the "calamity which [God was going to] bring on this place" (v. 20).

These two aspects of personal response indicate a heart that is open to God: humbling ourselves and seeking the Lord. How we respond to the Word of God will determine the whole direction of our lives from that moment on!

A sincere response to the Word of God is no small matter. There is a great difference between (on the one hand) simply reading the Scriptures and being interested in various opinions about the meaning of a text, and (on the other hand) wanting to know what God has said and responding faithfully and obediently to what God is saying to us personally through the Word. King Josiah was sincere.

But Josiah's response to the Word of God was not just deeply personal; it became *deliberately public* (23:1–25). In this incredible section of Scripture, we first see the king gathering together the leadership and all the people of Jerusalem. Then he read "in their hearing all the words of the Book of the Covenant" (23:2). What a scene this must have been! Second, after the hearing of the Word, we learn that "the king stood by a pillar and made a covenant before the LORD, to follow the LORD and to keep His commandments and His testimonies and His statutes, with all his heart and all his soul, to perform the words of this covenant that were written in this book. And all the people took a stand for the covenant" (v. 3). It started with the king's stand. He made public his commitment to the Lord and to the Word. Everyone knew what he stood for—literally! It is no surprise that the people followed such a leader in making a "stand for the covenant" (v. 3). So third, a covenant was made based upon the hearing of the words of God.

It would be premature to stop at this critical moment noted above and see this as the end of the "stand" taken. Actually this act of commitment was just the beginning—the beginning of a campaign to cleanse the land that was truly remarkable. As you read 2 Kings 23:4–25, you are amazed at the energy and perseverance of the king in seeking to rid the land of the sins and practices that were bringing on the wrath of God. There was removal of people associated with idolatry. There was bringing out, breaking down, burning, and defiling. There was tearing, cutting in pieces, and pulverizing. The action verbs throughout this account are instructive in and of themselves, indicating a practical, physical aspect to this cleansing of the nation following the covenantal commitment made. To be specific, Josiah did all this in order to "perform the words of the law which were written in the book that Hilkiah the priest found in the house of the LORD" (23:24). Thus, Josiah sought to deal with the sins and idolatry of the nation deliberately and thoroughly.

We have to ask ourselves how far we will go in order to obey what God has told us to do. Will we take a stand? Will we go as far as necessary to "clean house" to be what God wants us to be? Will we seek to influence those within our sphere of responsibility toward faithfulness to God and obedience to His Word? Josiah's commitment was complete, resulting in a serious cleansing of the land, the reading of which leaves us breathless. On the positive side, this campaign was accompanied by a celebration of the Passover that was unique in the history of Israel (vv. 21–23). God was honored and His saving work was remembered.

There was no king like Josiah in terms of his turning to the Lord "with all his heart, with all his soul, and with all his might" (v. 25). What a distinctive legacy, and what a contrast to King Solomon, whose heart turned away from the Lord.

These two examples not only help us understand matters of the heart, they reveal how serious matters of the heart truly are. The Christian leader's heart must be given to the Lord and must be responsive to God's Word. Faithfulness begins right there. The leader must guard the inner being, the heart of things. Awareness of the consequences of sin, a readiness to repent, and a wholehearted commitment to the Lord must be there. Alongside of these lessons from King Solomon's demise are the needs for humility before the Lord and an openness to His Word as we saw in Josiah's life. We need more Josiahs in our day—leaders whose hearts are turned toward the Lord, whose response to God is both deeply personal and deliberately public in impact.

On the practical level, I think it is important to recognize that this need to guard our hearts is a lifelong responsibility. Our inner being— our spiritual heart—must be strengthened in the Lord through the Word and by the Spirit. We must allow the Word to test our hearts and to examine our lives. We cannot assume that we will always be going forward in our walk with God. Much can happen in a day, in a moment in time, to turn our hearts away from undisputed love, commitment, and obedience to the Lord.

This won't be the last time we touch on this subject in a book dealing with faithfulness. But I hope these biblical examples will indicate the incredible importance of matters of the heart. The consequences alone of Solomon's heart trouble and, in contrast, the tender heart of Josiah ought to be enough to cause us to pray the following words:

Put a guard around my heart, O God. May I pursue You and Your will alone. Reveal the idols of my heart. Expose every sin. Keep my heart tender toward You, and may I continually obey You and be an influence for Your glory! I need You, Lord, and I invite You to use any and every means to enable me to live faithfully with an undivided heart. Amen.

CHAPTER 6

Contending for the Faith

JUDE 1-4, 17-25

Jude, who introduces himself in his letter as "Jude, a bondservant of Jesus Christ, and brother of James" (v. 1), was writing to Christians, calling them to "contend earnestly for the faith which was once for all delivered to the saints" (v. 3). Jude clearly stated that although he wanted to write about "our common salvation" (v. 3), he gave his attention—out of necessity—to alerting, instructing, exhorting, and inspiring these believers concerning the battle for faith and truth.

From the earliest days of the church, there has been a concern to believe the truth, proclaim the truth, teach the truth, defend the truth, and distinguish the truth from error. We need to view this letter as one of pastoral concern for the people of God. This is a letter written to believers in order to wake them up to the danger they are facing. This was not written to persuade nonbelievers of the validity of the Christian gospel. No, the concern was an "in-house" concern for the people of God—the danger of false teaching impacting the lives of individuals and the church as a whole.

Sadly the battle for truth is not fought in a vacuum, separated from life, people, personalities, and movements. No, the battle for truth and "the faith" is fought in the context of real people, real issues, real error, and real consequences. Jude's little letter is an example of this, as the authoritative writer pens God-breathed Scripture to help real people deal with a real situation.

I want us to look at this letter in an overview fashion to be challenged by Jude's straight teaching and exhortation. For we all are called to be defenders of the truth. Leaders are to protect the people of God, guiding them *with* the truth and *into* the truth. We will always be in a battle for the truth. Our present day is no exception.

The Necessity of the Fight

Just as Jude sensed the need to call his readers to the battle for truth, we need to acknowledge that this battle is a necessary one. Not all fights are right. There are plenty of battles fought "for the Lord's sake" that the Lord doesn't want anything to do with! But believers—especially Christian leaders—will need to be involved in this battle (2 Tim. 4:7). Truth is real, and so is error.

Jude sees the people he confronts as being "unnoticed." They had crept into the life of the church unawares and were already doing their perverting work. The urgency with which he writes is in light of the fact that some of God's people might not have even realized that subversive spiritual terrorism was taking place. Like termites, their destructive work was taking place without being seen or sensed. But the consequences would be serious if this hidden problem was not exposed.

Because of the evil one (the father of lies) and because of the sinfulness of man and the deceptive ways of men, there will always be the need to be alert and ready for attacks on the faith. So this fight is necessary for two reasons: the reality of truth and the reality of error. The fact that there is a "faith"—indeed "*the* faith," speaking of what is believed by Christians—there would need to be a defending of the truth in the light of non-truth (Jude 3). This truth we are talking about is not a matter of personal or cultural preference. Jude makes clear that he is talking about truth that is "once for all delivered" (v. 3).

Not only is this truth "once for all delivered," it is to be believed by the saints. This phrase "the saints" indicates that truth was not regional or sectarian; rather it is to be believed by all the saints. This is why we can refer to it as "*the* faith," the body of truth that is to be believed.

Thus, Jude is talking about absolute truth—the truth that God has revealed for His people to believe, know, and live by. This truth was certainly the teaching of the apostles of the Lord (v. 17). It surely had to do with the grace of God (v. 4), the Lord Jesus Christ (v. 4), and the "common salvation" (v. 3) of "those who are called, sanctified by God the Father, and preserved in Jesus Christ" (v. 1). It is safe to say that the truth Jude is defending is the apostles' doctrine, which ultimately would come down to us today in the New Testament.

In our day the battle for the faith continues, although the players, the personalities, the problems, the perversions, and the particulars may change. Are we ready? Do we stand on the alert? Or are we unwilling to stand, watch, and seek an awareness in order to detect the errors and perversions of truth that can emerge suddenly, subtly, and even secretly? Do we value the truth highly enough to study it in order to distinguish it from error? Today we have the privilege of having the complete canon of Holy Scripture available to us. The authoritative Word of God is to be studied and proclaimed so that the truth is known and believed.

The Enemy in the Fight

Much of Jude's letter is devoted to describing and denouncing the false teachers and their error. Being a specific letter, written to combat a specific problem, our discussion of this enemy will not cover all enemies or issues that are addressed here or in the New Testament. But I encourage you to read through the center part of Jude's letter (vv. 4–16), just to get a sense of Jude's concern and his description of the false teachers of his day. There is an interweaving of description and denouncement on the part of Jude, but let me summarize the picture he paints this way:

- From the standpoint of *truth*, the enemy was a perverter (v. 4).
- From the standpoint of *God*, the enemy was expected, condemned, and under judgment (v. 4).
- From the standpoint of *teaching*, the enemy was arrogant, manipulative, and self-centered (v. 15).

- From the standpoint of *lifestyle*, the enemy was ungodly, wrong in motives and in manner (vv. 16–18).
- From the standpoint of the *church*, the enemy was harmful, causing divisions (v. 19).
- From the standpoint of *spirituality*, the enemy was carnal, fleshly, and devoid of the Spirit (v. 19).

To put this in another way, these errorists were:
- perverters of grace (v. 4)
- condemned by God (v. 4)
- ones who denied our Lord Jesus Christ (v. 4)
- arrogant and manipulative in speech (v. 15)
- ungodly in lifestyle (vv. 16–18)
- harmful to the church (v. 19)
- carnal in spirituality (v. 19)

These enemies were people who failed the tests of mature and godly leaders and teachers. You get a sense of the self-centeredness, arrogance, and lack of submission to the Lord and authority that characterized these people. Ultimately what they taught, how they lived, and everything about them denied our only Master and Lord, Jesus Christ.

Watch out for the signs of such error and for errorists. One of the important rules of any fight, competition, or combat is to know how to distinguish the enemy. One of the roles of the Word of God is to reveal the enemy (and enemies) of the truth of the gospel. Furthermore, as we learn the truth and love the truth, we will be more sensitive to error.

I remember getting to know a Christian who, for a period of time before his conversion, had been a disciple of a guru in India. His conversion to Christ had taken place through the simple witness and lifestyle of missionaries and the personal reading of the Scriptures. What impressed me was the sensitivity of this man to truth and to the type of falsehood that had trapped him in his pre-conversion days. He shared with me the importance of the distinction between God the Creator and mankind as

God's creation. In other words, when you sense that there is a teaching that blurs the lines between who God is and who we are, you have to be careful. The false doctrine he believed right before his conversion did indeed blur these lines as he pursued "god-ness." It is one thing to talk about God's indwelling presence by the Holy Spirit, but it is another to speak of becoming god or uniting into the oneness that is god. God is wholly other than His creation, although God has revealed aspects of His character and attributes through His creation. Praise His name that we can be called the children of God because of God's grace, love, and the saving work of Christ. We are also to grow into the likeness of the Son of God, which is indeed God's purpose for us (Rom. 8:28–30). But these are clear doctrines taught in the Scriptures, which maintain the "otherness," the sovereignty, and other incommunicable attributes of God. We need to know the truth and love the truth so much that we can tell when it is being challenged, bent, or diluted by doctrines of unspiritual men.

To clarify, we are not talking about diversity and a variety of views on secondary matters within the body of Christ. Paul addresses this clearly in Romans 14:1–15:13. Disputable matters do exist between believers, and they should not be the cause of division, rejection, arrogance, and pressure within the family of God. Paul pleaded for love, acceptance, mutual respect, and unity despite differences in perspective and practice within the life of the church. But when someone touched the "truths of the gospel," as the Galatians discovered, they were in for a fight with the apostle.

Jude was concerned with basic truths that are part of the fabric of the faith we hold and for which we must die. But such truths, though perhaps heard in what these errorists were *saying*, were not being carried through in their lifestyle and manner of ministry. You cannot ultimately separate the teaching from the teacher. There is an incarnational reality to truth. What is taught must demonstrate itself in life, especially in the lives of those who teach. That is why so much time is given in this epistle to the lifestyle of these teachers of error. In actual fact, we read more about their ungodly lifestyle than about the specifics of their error. Good commentaries can give you more insight into the type of false teachings that were being perpetuated, but I want to stress here the importance of their manner of teaching, their lifestyle, and the divisiveness of their ministries.

The Strategy for the Fight

So what is to be our response? What is the strategy for this fight of faith? Here is where I want to place the most emphasis, because the nature of error will change from time to time, but I think the basic strategy presented here will serve us well throughout the years.

WE MUST EXPECT THE ENEMY

One of the enemy's greatest weapons is the element of surprise. We not only have Jude's letter to alert us to this but also the predictions of the apostles concerning the last days (see 2 Tim. 3:1–4:5). Furthermore, one could add that we have the weight and witness of the Scriptures themselves. So we need to actively remember what has been predicted, living in light of true expectations. We have already viewed Acts 20:28–31 in our study of Paul's farewell address. Note also these words of Jesus:

> Beware of false prophets, who come to you in sheep's clothing, but inwardly they are ravenous wolves. You will know them by their fruits. Do men gather grapes from thornbushes or figs from thistles? Even so, every good tree bears good fruit, but a bad tree bears bad fruit. A good tree cannot bear bad fruit, nor can a bad tree bear good fruit. Every tree that does not bear good fruit is cut down and thrown into the fire. Therefore by their fruits you will know them. (Matt. 7:15–20)

My father recounted on several occasions how a cult targeted his area of London when he was pastor of Duke Street Baptist Church in Richmond, England. He was so concerned that he chose to address the relevant truth matters directly from the pulpit, warning the people. My father sensed his pastoral responsibility to protect the flock, and God graciously preserved the church.

There must be an awareness of the errors of our own day and, sadly, of those who teach or promote them. It is not our job to be rude, crude, or belligerent in a non-Christian way, but we must not be naïve, negligent, or cowardly in being willing to clarify truth and expose error.

We Must Protect Ourselves

This might sound selfish, but it is anything *but* selfish. It is vital and critical. On numerous flights over the years, I have listened to the flight attendant's presentations concerning the safety features of the aircraft. Often if not always, when the oxygen masks are referred to, the adults are instructed specifically to put their masks on first before they put masks on their children or anyone else. Admittedly I have never asked the flight attendants why they give this instruction. But I think I know at least one reason: you will not be able to help anyone else, even your children, if you lose consciousness or have suffered the consequences of the lack of oxygen yourself. To make sure that you will be able to help others, you need to make sure that you are protected, that you have the supply of oxygen you need.

Jude called the saints to personal accountability and to a spiritual fitness that would enable them to withstand the enemy and be able to help others in desperate need of rescue. At the center of these directives is the command to "keep yourselves in the love of God" (v. 21). This speaks of the believers' responsibility to maintain their walk with God. Remember, Jude had already said (as he greeted these believers), "To those who are the *called*, sanctified by God the Father, and *preserved* for Jesus Christ: Mercy, peace, and love be multiplied to you" (vv. 1–2, emphasis mine). These same people who were to "keep" themselves had been "called" by God and were being *kept* by God. Here we see the balance of Scripture in relation to God's care for His people and our own responsibility to do those things necessary to guard our own lives and to grow.

God's children have their own responsibility to "walk" in the relationship they have with God. Throughout the Scriptures, God's people are urged to walk in faith and obedience, to live the life that God has called them to live. In so doing, the relationship with God is expressed and maintained. Jesus declared God's love for His disciples, but they were to "abide in [His] love" (John 15:9). At the practical level, this "abiding" calls for dependence and obedience on a daily, moment-by-moment level. We are to give heed to our walk with God, to live in the relationship of love we have with God.

Looking at these verses, I agree with The MacArthur Study Bible notes on the three surrounding participles that describe what is involved in this main imperative to "keep yourselves in the love of God."[1] This protection is sorely needed in light of the battle we face. Keeping yourselves in the love of God involves:

- "building yourselves up on your most holy faith" (v. 20)
- "praying in the Holy Spirit" (v. 20)
- "looking for the mercy of our Lord Jesus Christ unto eternal life" (v. 21)

"Building yourselves up on your most holy faith" speaks of being edified, strengthened, and established in the faith and on the foundation of the faith—"your most holy faith" (v. 20). There is never a time when we have finished learning or growing. There is never a time when we do not need protection. But what is involved practically in "building yourselves up on your most holy faith" (v. 20)?

The specifics are not given here, but I would suggest that Jude had in mind a continuous growth in knowledge of the truth and in depth of faith. This exhortation would be similar to that of the apostle Peter at the end of his second letter—to "grow in the grace and knowledge of our Lord and Savior Jesus Christ" (2 Pet. 3:18). Such things would seem to be in mind:

- *attention* to the truth taught and believed
- *application* of the truth taught and believed
- *action* on the truth taught and believed

Gleaning more from 2 Peter, which shares similar concerns with Jude, one would think that growth in character and conduct based on the truth would be a central aspect of Jude's strategy. Second Peter 1:1–11 spells out the need for growth on the part of those who are genuinely Christian. The potential for growth is clearly presented in verses 1–4. But then Peter calls for a pursuit of growth that builds on the faith that these believers have (vv. 5–7). He lists moral excellence, knowledge, self-control, perseverance, godliness, brotherly kindness, and love. These specifics may not have been in Jude's mind at all, but I think Jude was challenging his readers to do those things that would strengthen their faith and add to their faith. One could suggest various spiritual disciplines at this point, but I would suggest that these disciplines revolve around knowing the truth, learning more about the truth, and putting the truth into practice. Jude probably had the church context in mind in which believers strengthen one another in the truth. (For interesting parallels, see 1 Pet. 2:1–5 and Col. 2:6–10.)

Jude adds to this directive "praying in the Holy Spirit" (Jude 20). Whatever else this means, it speaks of spiritual prayer as a regular and critical part of our lives. The emphasis is probably on corporate prayer, although I'm sure personal and private prayer would not be discouraged! I know that the phrase "in the Holy Spirit" (v. 20) can imply a number of things, but let me try to view this within general New Testament teaching. The Holy Spirit who indwells us is the same Spirit who helps us in our weakness, by whom and with whom we pray (Rom. 8:26–27). Our need is to be in tune with the Holy Spirit and indeed to be enabled by the Holy Spirit.

Paul says elsewhere that we have access to God the Father through Christ "by one Spirit" (Eph. 2:18). The role of the Holy Spirit is critical to our fellowship with God. Just as we must live by the Spirit, and walk by the Spirit, we must pray in the Holy Spirit. This praying in the Holy Spirit is to be our regular duty. It is part of our protection in the battle for truth.

One of our greatest contemporary problems is prayerlessness in our busyness and pragmatic approach to life. Prayer needs to be a regular part of our strategy to fight the fight of faith, "praying always with all prayer and supplication in the Spirit, being watchful to this end with all perseverance and supplication for all the saints—and for me, that utterance may be given to me, that I may open my mouth boldly to make known the mystery of the gospel" (Eph. 6:18–19).

It is sad when a false dichotomy is drawn between the truth of the Scriptures and the work of the Holy Spirit. Jude emphasized the building of ourselves up in the faith, but then he moved directly to the matter of prayer in the Holy Spirit. We need to pray in the Spirit of Truth to be able to understand truth and apply it to our own lives. We need the protection of the Holy Spirit in the spiritual battle. Being born of the Spirit, baptized by the Spirit, sealed by the Spirit, led by the Spirit, walking in the Spirit, demonstrating the fruit of the Spirit, being filled by the Spirit, gifted by the Spirit, empowered or anointed by the Spirit—all of these biblical truths and experiences indicate that the Christian life is a life in the Holy Spirit. So one could hardly imagine prayer that is not in some way related to the work of the Holy Spirit in our lives. It is the Holy Spirit who knows the will of God and knows us through and through. The Spirit can enable us to pray as we ought in our weakness and in our ignorance of the specific will of God, which may be more often than we are willing to admit!

Having said what we have said about the Holy Spirit, there still is the need to pray. The Holy Spirit does not pray *instead* of us; He enables us to pray and intercedes on our behalf. Surely the Spirit helps us when we literally cannot pray due to weakness, but He doesn't pray when we refuse to pray or are too lazy to pray. Thus, prayer needs to be encouraged in our day, possibly as never before. Why? Because our self-sufficiency, our man-centeredness, our low expectations concerning the miraculous, our confidence in strategies, our busyness, and our sheer lack of true dependence upon God are barriers to meaningful dependent prayer.

Let's face it—we have habitual solutions for many issues in life without sensing the need for prayer. This is a dangerous position to be in. As we look at the church worldwide, it does seem that the church is exploding in those parts of the world where people are poor and needy and God is their only hope. We may be cynical about this situation, but this has been the norm if you take Paul's words seriously (1 Cor. 1:26–31). We pray because we desire such fellowship with God, and we pray because we are desperate to bring our lives and our needs before Him. The Holy Spirit is essential to the life and practice of prayer.

Jude gave further instruction concerning "protecting ourselves" in this battle for truth when he wrote that we are to be "looking for the mercy of our Lord Jesus Christ unto eternal life" (v. 21). We need to live in the light of the Lord's coming every day. It is the mercy of our Lord that should give us perspective and comfort as we live our lives.

As Paul summarized the grace of God in Titus 2:10–14, he included in his teaching the phrase, "looking for the blessed hope and glorious appearing of our great God and Savior Jesus Christ" (v. 13). The whole direction of one's life is impacted by what a person is looking and hoping for, what motivates the person to keep going forward in the same direction.

Jude challenged his readers not only to look forward eschatologically, but also to look to the Lord personally as their hope for mercy and deliverance. We need mercy ultimately and eternally, but we also need mercy daily. Don't we spend most of our time living day-by-day? We may be looking forward to that next big event on the human calendar: a graduation, a job, a marriage, a purchase, a promotion, a new experience, retirement, or some other phase of life. But a passionate longing for the merciful and glorious intervention of our Lord is dulled by the preoccupations, the cares, and the "good stuff" of life here and now. Oh, we get fascinated with speculative eschatology, but that is not the issue. Part of our spiritual protection is to place our hope and our expectation in the mercy we will experience when the Lord returns. Such a hope keeps us from being controlled by the priorities and pleasures of this world. This sounds like old-fashioned truth, and it may be! But whether it is old-fashioned or not, an eternal perspective, a longing for the coming of the Lord, and a hope in the Lord's mercy as our source of ultimate deliverance will keep us on track in the spiritual battle we are facing.

I'll never forget Bible teacher and author Dr. John Phillips sharing a statement something like this: "The most important decision a person will make is between heaven and hell. The second most important decision a person will make is between heaven and earth." It is easy to live for earth, to live for now. Eternity is not on the mind of most people as they go to work each morning. But the Christ-centered believer is looking and waiting for "the mercy of our Lord Jesus Christ unto eternal life" (Jude 21). Living with an eternal perspective, dependent upon the Lord and waiting on Him, keeps the believer in the center of God's will. Our hope needs to be fixed on the Lord, His grace, and His revelatory coming (1 Pet. 1:13). There is nothing to hope for in the shifting sands of this world. Our hope must be in the Lord and in His promised mercy toward us. Such a perspective will keep our priorities tied to eternity and to the Lord's priorities for us. In short, we as believers should live as if Christ died yesterday, rose this morning, and is coming back later today!

We Must Care for the Endangered

"And on some have compassion, making a distinction; but others save with fear, pulling them out of the fire, hating even the garment defiled by the flesh" (Jude 22–23).

This is a very difficult set of verses, due to textual issues, but the basic teaching is clear. As we face the battle of faith, we must be ready to help those who are hurting, struggling, and endangered in the battle. We are called to action—to care for people who need our help at their point of need.

Some have seen two groups of needy people here, and some have seen three groups. But all of the people in view need active ministry with love and compassion in order to be rescued from spiritual damage and/or death. Let's identify some groups that are at risk in the fight of faith.

• *The doubting.* "And on some have compassion, making a distinction" (Jude 22). The English Standard Version reads, "And have mercy on those who doubt" (see also the New American Standard, which reads, "And have mercy on some, who are doubting"). I believe this represents those who are struggling or wrestling with the faith, probably due to false teachers. We should not turn our backs on people who are not growing or are confused or troubled in their faith. Rather we should compassionately reach out in mercy to these people. We have received mercy from a God of mercy, and we need to extend mercy. Such people—doubters—can be frustrating to a church body and can be high maintenance for any pastor or leader. But we should not cut off such people. We should embrace them and, if possible, mentor them with mercy. This is a very important aspect of ministry. People who have been influenced by weak or false teaching need to be able to get help rather than feel they have no place to share their doubts, questions, and concerns.

Practically speaking, it is dangerous when people who are wrestling with spiritual/truth issues get isolated or separated from the fellowship of believers. Isolation provides a greater opportunity for false teaching to take root. Lack of accountability can lead to a lack of spiritual protection and a decrease in the very spiritual disciplines that enable growth to occur. When someone is not being built up in the faith, is not involved in prayer, and is not hoping in the Lord, spiritual drifting or disaster may be at hand. For those engaged in spiritual struggle, it is best to help them earlier rather than later.

• *The desperate.* "But others save with fear, pulling them out of the fire" (v. 23). The picture is of endangered people on the verge of being burned in the fires of judgment. Oh, what an important ministry this is! Let's recognize the consequence of false beliefs and the need to rescue the endangered. There are people who are on the edge all around us. We need to have eyes that can see and hearts that are open to those who are dangerously close to embracing falsehood and facing the consequences.

Surely this is an important aspect of the care and oversight of a Christian leader toward those they influence.

• *The defiled.* "And on some have compassion, making a distinction; but others save with fear, pulling them out of the fire, hating even the garment defiled by the flesh" (vv. 22–23). We are to help the sinner even though we hate the sin. Indeed, we are to help the sinner, hating the defilement of the flesh. Either this is a group similar to the "endangered" above, or these people are one step further toward serious trouble and consequences. They are already stained and impacted by the sins of the flesh. The person ministering to them has to be careful not to get sucked into the condition of these people, but must carefully seek to rescue them before it is too late.

What a picture of ministry! What a picture of mercy! What a need we have for merciful ministry!

I remember my wife, Ellen, helping a young lady who was involved in prostitution. Ellen arranged a rendezvous with this individual, literally to pick her up and get her out of her physical situation. Ellen was involved in a rescue operation. She was seeking to pull this person out of her situation without being influenced or "defiled" by the sinful practices and atmosphere that surrounded this person.

So we've seen the strategy in this fight of faith: expecting the enemy, protecting yourself, caring for the endangered. What does all this mean for leaders specifically?

Leaders need to take the battle for truth seriously. Leaders need to be aware of the dangers of false teaching and seek to be sensitive to contemporary lies and falsehoods that could impact the people under the leader's influence and care. Then the leader needs to think in terms of prevention and protection. This is an important aspect of the ministry of the church. Church activities are not just "fun and games," although the joy of the Lord needs to be present. We need to minister with the realization that we are in a spiritual war. Truth needs to be proclaimed clearly and helpfully so that error and falsehood can be sensed and seen for what it is. This is one of the reasons why we need the regular proclamation of scriptural truth and the teaching of the Bible and its doctrines. Not everyone can be an expert on cults, deceitful philosophies, false religions, etc., but believers need to be taught the truth. The preaching and teaching ministries of the church are not entertainment. They are provided and practiced to keep believers spiritually healthy or to bring them back to spiritual health.

Leaders need to help their people develop good spiritual practices and disciplines that will help them walk in the truth. Personal reading of the Word of God and the importance of prayer need to be emphasized. The doctrines of Christ need to be taught, including the need to live in the light of the mercy of the Lord and His coming. These are basic aspects of church life, teaching, and practice.

Finally, leaders need to be involved regularly in rescue operations of one type or another. There are people all around us influenced and impacted by false teaching and error. The immediate consequences are real and the stakes are high and eternal. We need to be sensitive to the doubts of people wrestling with ideas, philosophies, religions, and error. We need to be ready to go after those who are on the edge of destruction, recognizing the seriousness of their situation. There are times when the ninety and nine must be left in order to go after the one that has wandered away and is in serious danger. Leadership calls for this. This is a major part of ministry.

Victory in the Fight

It is appropriate to ask, "Is there hope for this battle? Is the outcome uncertain? Are we unsure of any kind of victory?" Well, Jude ends on a glorious note of certainty. "Now to Him who is able to keep you from stumbling, and to present you faultless before the presence of His glory with exceeding joy, to God our Savior, who alone is wise, be glory and majesty, dominion and power, both now and forever. Amen" (vv. 24–25).

Jude had confidence that God was able to keep His people and see them through to eternity. Though the issues in this battle are real and critical and eternal, God is committed to seeing us through victoriously. This well-known doxology is beautiful, glorious, and rich in words and thought. But it is even *more* beautiful when seen in the context of this epistle, viewing it in two movements:

What God Is Able to Do

The battle is tough, the dangers are real, the casualties hurt, and the ultimate stakes are high. But God is able to guard us, to keep us from "stumbling." In this regard, it is good to remember Paul's question: "If God is for us, who can be against us?" (Rom. 8:31). Although Paul is addressing another aspect of God's work, the principle is ultimately the same. We can fight the fight of faith, knowing that the God who is able is the one who guards and keeps us. Yes, we have our responsibilities, but our dependency is upon Him, and He is able.

God is also able to "present" us (v. 24)—to present us "faultless." This is what God is working toward in our lives. This faultlessness is due to what God has done for us in Christ, and what He is doing to keep us "until that Day" (2 Tim. 1:12) when we meet our Lord and stand in His presence.

Who God Is

This One who is able is described in a beautiful flow of words and phrases: He is our Savior. He alone is wise. He is due all glory, majesty, dominion, and power, now and forever. God is sufficient. He is worthy of our faith, and He is in complete control as the sovereign God.

So instead of ending on a pessimistic note, Jude takes us into the glorious presence of God Himself. Victory in the fight of faith is not just a matter of human effort and activity. No, God Himself is involved. The sovereign Savior has committed Himself to see us through, and He is able to keep us through the fight, presenting us faultless before His presence. And note that this is going to take place "with exceeding joy" (v. 24). These are words of confident assurance for those who are fighting the fight of faith.[2]

As we conclude this chapter, it is helpful to remember that this letter from Jude could be described as an "emergency letter." Jude is concerned because of an unnoticed danger, and he wants everyone to be aware of this danger to truth and to know what to do about it. This in itself is instructive. This letter comes from a leader disturbed and concerned.

There will always be the need for an apologetic thrust in faithful ministry. Truth has to be defended. Our people need to be protected. There is no time to waste when we sense that real falsehood is on the loose. Therefore, it would be wise to evaluate our leadership and ministry activities from the standpoint of truth. Do we really sense that we are in a battle for truth, the faith, and for people's lives? As leaders, we need to maximize our time and efforts around those activities and relationships that have eternal significance.

CHAPTER 7

Pursuing Right Relationships

PHILEMON 4–20

It is the purpose of God to bring us into right relationship with Himself, and to form a community of believers who are in right relationship with one another. Relationships are not just necessary to accomplish certain mutual goals; right relationships are one of the primary goals of God in the life of the church. Therefore, right relationships must be a primary goal for the Christian leader.

You cannot read the Scriptures without sensing the importance of right relationships in general and especially among the people of God. We are to love God and to love our neighbor—two commandments that are inextricably linked together (Matt. 22:34–40). In other words, love for God will be seen in love for others (1 John 4:20–21). These are lifelong commitments that must be embraced by obedient children of God.

You see the importance of these truths in the Old Testament. Likewise, these truths are important in the New Testament as we see the forming of a "fellowship" that is in faith-union with the crucified-risen Christ and united by the Holy Spirit. Each person within this community is linked to one another as members in a body (Rom. 12:3–8), each contributing to the overall unity, ministry, and growth of this group of people who are in Christ. And those who lead are to do so with "diligence" (12:8), serving the goals of the body.

Ephesians 4:1–16 spells this out in more detail. The church is to be a community (one body, with Christ being the Head) where mutual ministry takes place in order that the members move toward being united in "the faith," growing toward maturity. The church should be an inter-related group of people actively edifying one another in love. Leaders and ministers are given to the church to bring about these important goals through Christ: unity, ministry, and maturity. Adding traits like humility, purity, and love, we cover most of the key words having to do with the nature and goals of the corporate life of the church.

I say all this to emphasize that good relationships are critical to the purpose of God; therefore, leaders must give a high priority to relational matters, especially within the life of the church. There are numerous examples of relational issues being addressed within the Scriptures, but one example that has spoken to me over the years is found in the amazing letter we know as Philemon. This letter is the communication of a leader who has chosen to get involved in a church fellowship and relationship matter. The letter reveals the apostle Paul's initiative to act purposefully, "for love's sake" (Philem. 9), in a situation needing reconciliation.

Paul was in chains. And in this restricted condition, he wrote to a house church, especially to the leadership of this church—Philemon, Apphia, and Archippus. It becomes evident that he was writing on behalf of a man named Onesimus, whom Paul was sending back to Philemon and the church. Reading between the lines, it would seem that Onesi-mus was a slave who had left Philemon's household and had somehow ended up with Paul in Rome (or wherever Paul was at that time).

Some background information can be gleaned from Colossians 4:7–18, a letter probably written about the same time, which mentions Onesimus. Whether Onesimus stole something is not clear, but being a slave, he was in danger in the Roman world. Yet Onesimus became very special to Paul. It appears that Paul may have led him to faith in Christ, and that Onesimus had helped Paul in his present condition. Indeed, it sounds as if Paul would have liked Onesimus to stay with him and help him. But there was a matter that needed attention. There was unfinished business. Onesimus needed to be in a right relationship with Philemon and the church because of what had taken place.[1]

This was obviously a very important matter to Paul. And as we view how he handled the situation, we see a loving leader carefully and skillfully seeking to bring about a solution to a serious social and relational problem. We will see, first of all, how Paul presents a personal exhortation for Christian love to be practiced in this situation. Then we will journey back through the 335 Greek words of this letter to appreciate the personal example of Christian love that Paul displays himself.[2]

The Personal Exhortation for Christian Love

This letter is an extended *parakalo*. It is a carefully written personal exhortation penned with passion and wisdom. After Paul's characteristic salutation, he moves into his thanksgiving and prayer (vv. 4–7), which is a regular feature in his letters. Often, an insight into Paul's concern in the letter is stated directly or sensed as you read these early parts of his letters.

> I thank my God, making mention of you always in my prayers, hearing of your love and faith which you have toward the Lord Jesus and toward all the saints, that the sharing of your faith may become effective by the acknowledgment of every good thing which is in you in Christ Jesus. For we have great joy and consolation in your love, because the hearts of the saints have been refreshed by you, brother. (Philem. 4–7)

Before Paul presents his exhortation, he shares words of appreciation and affirmation. Love and faith are mentioned with thanksgiving, while Paul's prayer request focuses on the "sharing" of their faith, pointing to the need for the active demonstration of their faith through "every good thing which is in you" (vv. 5–6). This difficult phrase seems tied to what Paul says next, pointing to the key issue in the letter: "For we have great joy and consolation in your love, because the hearts of the saints have been refreshed by you, brother" (v. 7). Paul is affirming the very quality that he is going to call into action in his exhortation. Now it is Paul's turn to be refreshed by Philemon's love, which will take place as Philemon responds to Paul's "heart" expressed in this powerful letter (v. 20).

It is important to observe that Paul deliberately chose to *appeal* to Philemon in this letter rather than to command him. Verses 8–9 reveal that Paul chose his method of presentation very carefully. By referring to himself as "Paul, the aged, and now also a prisoner of Jesus Christ" (v. 9), he was telling Philemon and his readers both what he *was* going to do and what he was *not* going to do. He would not be using his apostolic authority to compel Philemon to do something. Rather he was appealing on a personal, relational level and for love's sake. We know that Philemon and the church knew full well who Paul was, and they probably had a high regard for his authority. But if we take the text at face value, we have to recognize Paul's relational approach.

Considering the character or manner of Paul's exhortation, note his positive anticipation of a good response to what he desires (vv. 20–22). Indeed, Paul even used the word "obedience" in this closing part of his appeal, even though he had not approached Philemon in terms of an apostolic directive.

We can take notes on Paul here. The reason why he is proceeding in this fashion will become even more apparent as we go further along. The point here, though, is to learn from Paul's wise words and his relational approach, given the nature of the issue at stake.

What Paul Wants: The Five Rs

What was Paul actually trying to accomplish? One could simply say that Paul was trying to clear the slave's name and possibly release him to help Paul in future service. But let's look more carefully at the priority concerns behind Paul's intervention in this situation.

First of all, there is no question that Paul wanted the *right thing* to be done. As he stated in verse 8, "what is fitting" is what he is after, and that is referred to as "obedience" in verse 21. Even though Paul approached this situation personally and relationally, Paul was not unsure of God's will or of what needed to be done. He wanted right and righteousness to prevail. Relational matters can get complicated, and it is easy to lose sight of the "right" that needs to be done. Paul based his whole approach on what he believed was right, what must be done.

At the same time, Paul wanted Onesimus to be *restored* to fellowship with Philemon and the church. Restoration was needed because of the vulnerability of Onesimus in this situation. Onesimus may have been in Philemon's "bad book." He may have done wrong to Philemon in one way or another. Paul affirmed his paternal love for Onesimus, clearing Onesimus's name, explaining why he was sending him back, giving Philemon his own eternal perspective on the whole situation, then seeking complete acceptance and forgiveness for him if anything needed to be dealt with. This is a clear attempt to restore a "new brother" to fellowship in the life of a family and church. Given the sociocultural dynamics of this situation, we are seeing a radical gospel at work. Love is the principle of operation, which calls for restoration to be offered.

The third R is *reconciliation*. Onesimus was in a position of needing restoration. But the parties needed reconciliation to lead to right relationships within the fellowship of the church. Here we see the same apostle who was concerned about his relationship with the Corinthian church, showing the same kind of concern for reconciliation within the life of Philemon's house church. Paul put his own name and reputation on the line to see this reconciliation take place. This was obviously no small matter. It could not be swept under the carpet. It had to be dealt with face-to-face, especially given the social dynamics of the day.

If one is looking for the bottom line in Paul's exhortation, it is complete acceptance, a Christian reception for Onesimus as he returns (vv. 12, 17), and total forgiveness of any debt owed (vv. 18–19). These directives on Paul's part were the essentials for restoration and reconciliation to take place. The change in relational dynamics could not take place without action and cost.

It may sound simple from our vantage point, but how often in our day does relational discord continue because the necessary costly actions do not take place? Paul did everything in his power to encourage, appeal, and exhort the right things to happen so that personal restoration and corporate reconciliation would take place. And if Paul was trying to release Onesimus to help him in the ministry (vv. 13–14), he was seeking to go about it in the most complete and appropriate way to honor the Christian relationships and "social protocol" that would make such service possible and above reproach.

The fourth R is Paul's own *refreshment* (v. 20). I mention this because it is part of Paul's appeal. Philemon was known for his refreshing love toward the saints, and now Paul wanted to see this quality exercised in a way that would refresh Paul's "heart in the Lord" (v. 20). You can see how carefully Paul wrote this letter and how compelling his exhortation was when you put all the pieces together.

We have not drawn attention yet to an important part of Paul's exhortation in verses 14–16. Here is where we gain insight into why Paul was handling this situation as he did. Yes, he wanted a "good deed" to be done (v. 14). Yes, he wanted restoration, reconciliation, and personal refreshment to take place. But Paul's approach to all these matters was guided by something that we must grasp firmly. Paul wanted Philemon's actions to be "voluntary" and not by "compulsion" (v. 20). Also, if Paul was asking for the *release* of Onesimus to help him in ministry—the fifth R—he needed Philemon's consent for this to take place. One could say that Paul was working within the cultural norms and systems of the day, and I would not have any problem with that. It is wise to handle things within the appropriate cultural channels, if the Word of God is not being compromised. But I think there is something more here. Issues of restoration, reconciliation, and possible release could not be handled without the "heart issues" being dealt with. In other words, what needed to take place had to take place on the basis of Christian love, not by a power play of apostolic authority. Yes, Paul reminded Philemon that he owed him his life (v. 19), which probably meant his conversion to Christ. But behind these remarks were relational-spiritual dynamics that are fundamental to this whole letter.

The writer of 1 Corinthians 13 believed what he wrote. Love must prevail in this and every situation. Furthermore, a Christian perspective on this whole matter must be seen. That is why Paul had his "perhaps" statements, which sound unusual for him: "For perhaps he departed for a while for this purpose, that you might receive him forever, no longer as a slave but more than a slave—a beloved brother, especially to me but how much more to you, both in the flesh and in the Lord" (Philem. 15–16). I believe Paul wanted Philemon to see that there was a greater principle at stake here, not just the usual dynamics of a slave being restored to his master's household and then possibly released. More than that, there is a "forever" relationship (v. 15). More than a slave-master relationship, there is a brother-brother relationship within the love of God (v. 16).

How Philemon heard these words and what he did with them is not a matter of solid historical record. But one has to come to grips with the radical nature of Paul's thoughts here. Philemon could not view this situation simply on an economic or sociopolitical level any longer. This could not be viewed simply on a work-relation basis. Paul was calling for an approach based on Christian love. Christian love demanded certain things to take place, hopefully voluntarily, as Philemon understood the principle of love that was to operate in this relational/social problem.

As I view this letter, there is something deeper and richer that needs our attention. We have touched on it, but it needs full consideration now. Paul appealed for Christian love to be demonstrated in this complex relational situation. He framed his exhortation carefully, appealing on the basis of love, clearly stating what he would like to see happen, and supporting his requests with an eternal love-based perspective, which ultimately is the nature of fellowship or relationships in Christ. But Paul expressed and demonstrated this same Christian love himself within the letter. His exhortation is accompanied by Paul's own example of Christian love, demonstrated incarnationally in the very way he expressed himself in this letter.

The Personal Example of Christian Love

When we speak of Paul's example of love, we are not so much thinking about Paul's love for Philemon. Rather we are focusing on Paul's love for Onesimus. Keep in mind this is the apostle Paul—the principal human figure in the book of Acts. This is the man who wrote Romans and most of the epistles in the New Testament. This is the man who has framed Christian thought and theology since the first century. This is the man who blasted the apostle Peter for hypocrisy. This man did miracles, preached the gospel, planted churches, taught converts, trained leaders, risked his life for the gospel, and pioneered early Christian mission. This man, the apostle to the Gentiles, was putting his name and reputation on the line for a slave who was probably considered "useless" at that time by those to whom he wrote.

What are some of the ways Paul expressed his love for Onesimus?

First, we see Paul *commending* Onesimus. He reveals that this man is a "son" to Paul, which is probably more than a term of endearment. It probably refers to Onesimus's new relationship to Paul as a Christian, a spiritual son in the faith. But Paul goes further. He speaks highly of Onesimus, regardless of what Philemon and the church thought of him. There is every indication that Onesimus was considered "unprofitable" by Philemon, which was opposite of the meaning of his very name. Paul clearly stated that this man was now profitable both to Philemon and to Paul himself (v. 11). Paul took on the role of an advocate, speaking well of this man when he was in need of a "good word." Saying a good word on someone's behalf, especially if they are misunderstood or not appreciated, is a real ministry. Paul's words were few and simple, but they spoke volumes in the context of this letter. And a personal commendation from the pen of the apostle Paul was not something that could be taken lightly!

We see Paul's love also in his *willingness to sacrifice* his own desire to keep Onesimus with him—on the altar of higher principle! Paul said he was sending Onesimus back even though he would like to keep him there with him. Remember, Paul was "in chains," whatever that means exactly. Paul had his own needs. There was a sense in which Onesimus could have helped Paul on behalf of Philemon. If Paul was just going to do what was best for himself for the immediate future, he could have kept Onesimus with him. He probably had greater needs than Philemon did anyway! But Paul knew what was best for Onesimus and for Philemon. So instead of putting his own immediate needs first, Paul acted on principle, which ultimately was the principle of Christian love toward both Onesimus and Philemon. This also opened the door for reconciled relationships and future ministry as the Lord would lead. Much more could be said, trying to read between the lines, but the facts are clear.[3] Paul was willing to sacrifice immediate personal help to deal with this matter faithfully and to gain a long-term solution.

One of the most striking aspects of this letter is Paul's *identification* with Onesimus. Paul's advocacy role was not done at arm's length. He identified fully with his son in the faith, "begotten while in my chains" (v. 10). Regardless of the textual issues in verse 12, you sense Paul's love for Onesimus in the phrase "my own heart." But the kicker for me is found in verse 17. Paul says, "If then you count me as a partner, receive him as you would me."

What a statement and directive! Do you think Philemon considered himself to be in fellowship with Paul? Do you think he would have received Paul into the fellowship of the church? How do you think Philemon would have done so? Unlovingly? Disrespectfully? Casually? No, I don't think so. Philemon owed Paul his life, according to this letter. Philemon surely had a great appreciation for him. Paul was saying, "When Onesimus comes through your door, it's like it is me. Give him the same treatment you would give me." These are strong and loving words—loving words for Onesimus; strong words for Philemon and the church. I wonder if Onesimus ever read these words. What must it have meant to him to know that he had the personal love and reputation of the apostle Paul to rest in as he went back to Philemon and the church. Paul was willing to use the respect he should receive to help a brother who may not have been treated the same way.

There is one more evidence of love that needs to be mentioned, and that is found in verses 18–19: "But if [Onesimus] has wronged you or owes anything, put that on my account. I, Paul, am writing with my own hand. I will repay." Paul pens in his own handwriting his willingness to pay the bill for anything Onesimus owes Philemon. Now one might think that Paul is only posturing at this point, knowing that Philemon would not charge Paul for such matters. But we don't know that for sure. And in any case, what we need to see is that Paul wanted all offenses in this matter covered and cleared. He did not want any wrongs or debts outstanding as such. He was seeking complete righteousness, restoration, reconciliation, and release from whatever might have been owed on the part of Onesimus.

Boy, if I were a preacher, I might start preaching at this point! Does this scene not remind you of something, of Someone? Do you not sense Calvary's love flowing into this relational situation? Is not the touch of the Savior sensed in this situation? Are we not recipients of His advocacy, His identification, and His own payment of our sin debt? Is this not Christlike love operating on the horizontal level in human relationships? I think it is. Martin Luther wrote, "Here we see how Paul layeth himself out for poor Onesimus, and with all his means pleadeth his cause with his master, and so setteth himself as if he were Onesimus, and had himself done wrong to Philemon. Even as Christ did for us with God the Father, thus also doth Paul for Onesimus with Philemon. We are all his Onesimi, to my thinking."[4]

The Paul who wrote Romans 5:1–11 and 8:31–39 is the same Paul who wrote Philemon. And here in this letter we see the love of Christ demonstrated by the apostle Paul in the way he acts on Onesimus's behalf, for the good of all and for the furtherance of the gospel. Thank God for this Scripture that calls for Christian love to be exercised where true reconciliation was needed. But thank God also for the example shown to us through Paul, who revealed the very love he was calling for in the life of the early church.

Some Implications

1. The Christian leader must take seriously and address directly any relational issues and problems in life and ministry. This "slice of life" letter reveals the importance of this personal matter to the apostle Paul. I realize this letter was not written specifically to be a model or a course for future leaders. But having said that, this is a letter from a leader to leaders (and a church) exhorting them to deal with a relationship and fellowship matter. Thus, if nothing else is gleaned from this letter, we should gain an appreciation for the importance of dealing with these kinds of relational issues.

2. The critical roles of mediator, advocate, reconciler, and instructor are all potential and necessary roles for the leader. Given the variety of relational situations and issues that leaders will face, it is almost certain that the leader will need to initiate action to bring about potential relational change. This will call for the adopting of one or all of the roles we've mentioned. When filling one of these roles, the Christian leader is following not only in the footsteps of Paul but also in the path of our Lord and Savior, Jesus Christ.

3. It is clear that Paul handled this matter very carefully and intentionally. Besides adopting the approach of a personal appeal, the letter is worded tactfully and purposefully. The leader needs to pray for wisdom and must seek to be a tactful communicator in any relational matter. The goal is always righteousness—the "right things" being done, resulting in right relationships. But for this to happen, wisdom and sensitivity are needed to guide those involved through the necessary processes to get to the right solution, by God's grace.

4. If you put yourself in the shoes of Philemon, an application can be transferred (with sensible adjustments) to your own situation when someone is in need of restoration and reconciliation with you personally. Whatever other factors are involved, the Christian must be willing to receive, accept, and forgive as a way of restoration and reconciliation. There may be many "okay, but-what-ifs"—in work and other settings—but we need to let the radicalness and simplicity of this letter speak to

us before we explain it all away with exceptions. The Christian must be willing to forgive on the personal level, and the Christian leader must always be seeking restoration and reconciliation, whatever other realities exist in the situation.

5. Personal sacrifice may be called for in order to address a relational situation in the best possible way for all involved. The apostle would have liked to have kept Onesimus with him, but there was the greater need for Onesimus to return to Philemon and for matters to be handled rightly for all parties involved. The leader needs to make sure that his or her personal needs are not getting in the way of the real solution to a problem.

6. The leader needs to have "big picture" thinking in addressing relational issues and matters. Paul straightforwardly sought to help Philemon see the big picture in this situation by comparing the temporary parting of Onesimus from Philemon to the "forever" relationship that would begin when Onesimus would be received into fellowship (v. 15). Likewise, the brother relationship (in Christ) with Onesimus was going to impact how Philemon was to view Onesimus the slave, how he was to receive him, release him from any debt, and possibly allow him to "minister" to Paul (or with Paul) in the future (v. 16). The apostle does not expound at length on the principles of Christian fellowship, but enough is said to guide Philemon in the right direction, especially when Paul's own example is kept in mind. It is so easy to cave in to lesser goals when handling such issues.

As we conclude viewing this aspect of faithfulness in the life of the leader, we need to think about three key words that should be a part of our thinking as we deal with relational and fellowship matters. "Grace" and "peace" are the usual words found in Pauline salutations (see v. 3). These two words are critical to understanding Christian fellowship and relationships. Grace certainly is the force that is active in true Christian fellowship. God has acted in grace toward us in Christ, and we are to do the same in our relationships. Without grace, we will not move in the direction of restoration, reconciliation, and forgiveness. Likewise, peace is what should characterize relationships within the local church. It is a primary goal in community life. Peace involves both relational activity and harmony based on grace.

Yet we must stress again the key word in relational matters—"love." Love based on truth seeks to achieve righteousness in relationships. Having said this, love's manner is guided by grace, and its goal is true peace for the glory of Christ. God's relationship with us is the pattern to follow, of course, especially as we view how God has expressed His love in Christ for us. Such love is not just a nice idea in a tough world. It is God's will for our lives. Anything less is disobedience.[5]

CHAPTER 8

Persevering in the Will of God

NEHEMIAH 6:1–19

After the great and glorious years of David and Solomon, after the divided kingdom period, after the two exiles of the Northern and Southern Kingdoms due to sin and disloyalty, after the return of many of God's people to Jerusalem and the surrounding country—when Israel was still under foreign control—something monumental happened in Sushan, Persia. While serving as "cupbearer" for King Artaxerxes during the middle of the fifth century BC, a man named Nehemiah received a tragic report concerning the condition of Jerusalem—both its people and its walls. The people were in trouble and disgrace, the walls broken down and the gates burned.

Nehemiah wept and prayed. He sought the Lord to make a way for him to return to Jerusalem to give himself to his people and this project (Neh. 1:1–11).

God wonderfully opened the opportunity for Nehemiah to travel to Jerusalem, and He protected him on his journey. The "hand of God" was with Nehemiah (a key phrase appearing in this marvelous biblical book; see Neh. 2:8). Opposition is mentioned from the very start (2:10), which would present itself in various ways throughout the account. Chapters 2–5 of Nehemiah tell of his arrival in Jerusalem, his inspection of the walls, the start of the rebuilding project, the rise of the opposition, and the continuation of the project. Chapter 5 gives choice insights into his integrity and compassionate leadership. Then chapter 6, where I want to focus, brings us to the final days of the rebuilding of the walls and gates project.

As we look at this matter of doing God's will, the early chapters of Nehemiah make it clear that this "work" Nehemiah was doing was, in fact, the will of God. This was a God project. The need was there. There was reproach rather than glory in the land. The need was shared with Nehemiah, and Nehemiah sought the Lord in fervent prayer. God gave him a specific answer to prayer and a way to Jerusalem. The hand of God was with Nehemiah. I say all this because not all of the activities Christians seek to perform are automatically the purposeful will of God. The will of God needs to be discerned and proven by a godly or renewed mind (Rom. 12:1–2). Nehemiah was such a man—a great example of a leader with a passion for the will of God.

The book of Nehemiah is not only or ultimately about Nehemiah himself. The book is about the God of Nehemiah and God's work in rebuilding His city and His people, just as He is always at work doing His will for His glory and on behalf of His purpose and people. In fact, this is exactly where a Christian leader should find himself or herself—not thinking about what we can do for God in fulfilling some personal agenda but rather discerning the will of God, and then doing that will with God's leading and enabling.

What we are going to focus on in this chapter is the fact that Nehemiah and the people of God had to face strong opposition in doing the will of God. Having an easy go of it—in any sense of the term—is not necessarily a sign of being in the center of God's will. The will of God may involve all sorts of trouble, including personal danger and death. That's why, among other reasons, there is such a need for a passionate commitment to the will of God.

Many truths about doing God's will surface in this specific chapter of Scripture, but I want us to focus on three that will help define what faithfulness to the will of God will involve.[1]

Destructive Strategies Faced When Doing God's Will

Now it happened when Sanballat, Tobiah, Geshem the Arab, and the rest of our enemies heard that I had rebuilt the wall, and that there were no breaks left in it (though at that time I had not hung the doors in the gates), that Sanballat and Geshem sent to me, saying, "Come, let us meet together among the villages in the plain of Ono." But they thought to do me harm. (Neh. 6:1–2)

Almost certainly, opposition will be experienced when doing God's will. The individuals Sanballat, Tobiah, and Geshem were leading figures in the surrounding region. Sanballat appears to have been the governor of Samaria, Tobiah may have been another area governor, and Geshem a leading or influential figure. Who they were precisely is not critical to the truths of the text, since the Scripture does not give us expanded information about their identities. What matters in this account is that they opposed the clear will of God. They were against someone who "had come to seek the well-being of the children of Israel" (2:10), someone who had been led by God's hand to rebuild the wall. So this opposition was not only opposition to a rebuilding project; it was opposition to God and His people. Let's look at the various attempts made in Nehemiah 6 to thwart the completion of the rebuilding project. Direct attack had been threatened earlier, but here we read of deceit, intrigue, and crafty attempts to thwart God's will.

THE STRATEGY TO DISTRACT AND DESTROY

Two of the neighboring leaders tried to arrange a meeting with Nehemiah. Indeed the text tells us that they sent a message four times to try to get Nehemiah to stop the work and come to a place where they could deal with him. They sought to distract Nehemiah and get him off the job, but the ultimate purpose seemed to be to destroy him.

I love Nehemiah's response, "I am doing a great work, so that I cannot come down. Why should the work cease while I leave it and go down to you?" (v. 3). It is clear that Nehemiah read their motives and knew they wanted to do him harm. Thus, he did not give in to their subtle plan. But this was not the end of the opposition. It rarely is. Plan B went into operation:

The Strategy to Disturb and Discourage

A false letter was presented to Nehemiah, saying that he was making himself "king in Judah" (v. 7) and that this would be reported to the king of Persia. This was a serious charge if it were true. Judah was in a very vulnerable position, and acts of treason or attempts to rise politically in opposition to the Persian Empire would not be tolerated.

Nehemiah's response was direct and confident: "No such things as you say are being done, but you invent them in your own heart" (v. 8). The text goes on to say, "For they all were trying to make us afraid, saying, 'Their hands will be weakened in the work, and it will not be done'" (v. 9). Nehemiah took strength in the truth and in the knowledge that this was a direct attempt to stop the work and will of God from being done. Fear can so easily lead to discouragement. Then one's heart for the will of God is weakened and the work suffers.

It is interesting to note that verse 9 ends with Nehemiah's prayer directly in response to the enemies' strategy: "Now therefore, O God, strengthen my hands." One has to be cautious in building principles on the basis of Old Testament examples. But I believe we are on safe ground to recognize the faithfulness of Nehemiah in how he responded to the opposition he faced. Here we see him praying specifically in the light of the opposition faced. Is that not a good example for us?

I once heard Charles Stanley share with a group of ministers the need to fight your battles in the prayer closet on your knees. There are certainly other aspects to spiritual warfare and defending the truth, but prayer needs to be fundamental and primary in our strategy. Nehemiah was a man of prayer, as we have already seen.

THE STRATEGY TO DECEIVE AND DISCREDIT

This third strategy was a little more complicated. A secret informer attempted to get Nehemiah to flee into the temple to save his life. Fleeing would have shown Nehemiah to be a coward and also would have caused him to do something inappropriate, since he was not someone with temple privileges. To do such a thing would have been an act of fear and a sin. Nehemiah refused to go into the temple. It is important to note his perception of their ultimate motive: "For this reason he was hired, that I should be afraid and act that way and sin, so that they might have cause for an evil report, that they might reproach me" (v. 13). Is it not the case that the work of God's servants has often been hindered or even halted by giving in to sin? The resultant discrediting often renders individuals unable to continue the work.

Dr. Hershael York has used the picture of mountain climbing to illustrate the fact that the higher you go in leadership, the more costly your errors. When you get into thinner air nearer the top of the mountain, little mistakes have bigger consequences.[2] Moses ended up not being able to lead the people into the land because of his sin "at the waters of Meribah Kadesh" (Deut. 32:51; Num. 20:1–13). Numerous other biblical examples could be given, but in Nehemiah we have an example of someone with the discernment to see the strategies and motives at work, someone able to say no and resist the schemes of the enemy.

Again, the scene ends with Nehemiah in prayer, committing his enemies into God's hands: "My God, remember Tobiah and Sanballat, according to these their works, and the prophetess Noadiah and the rest of the prophets who would have made me afraid" (6:14).

We need to be alert to the fact that there will be opposition to the purposes and will of God. If one strategy doesn't work, another will sometimes be used. Yes, we are in a spiritual war. The will of God is not done within a neutral environment. We must be self-controlled and alert. Behind the strategies of men is the enemy, "the devil [who] walks about like a roaring lion, seeking whom he may devour" (1 Pet. 5:8). We need to heed the words of Peter when he says, in the following verse,

"Resist him, steadfast in the faith, knowing that the same sufferings are experienced by your brotherhood in the world" (1 Pet. 5:9).

Has God given you a vision as he gave Nehemiah? Has He challenged you to do something you know for certain is His will? Have you made a commitment to Him to see something through to completion? Don't be surprised, then, if difficulties emerge or opposition arises.

There is a spiritual war that still must be fought (Eph. 6:10–20). This is part of the cost of doing the will of God. The wonderful thing is that Nehemiah was not distracted, discouraged, discredited, or destroyed. He overcame with God's help.

But it is *how* he overcame that is worthy of our attention now. There are no secrets in this matter of being an overcomer, but it certainly merits our attention to learn from Nehemiah's example.

Personal Qualities Needed When Doing God's Will

Nehemiah was totally committed to God and His will. He probably could have prayed the prayer my father heard Bobby Richardson, the New York Yankee great, pray at a public occasion: "Oh God, Your will—nothing more, nothing less, nothing else."

But let's look specifically at Nehemiah and the qualities he displayed. God was able to use him. God's will was done under his leadership. How would you characterize Nehemiah under the hand of God?

A MAN OF DETERMINATION

He didn't just *hear* about a problem in Jerusalem; he prayed. He didn't just *pray*; he spoke when he was given opportunity. He didn't just *speak*; he literally moved out and forward toward Jerusalem. He not only arrived at Jerusalem; he organized the rebuilding project. He went even further than this—He sought renewal and reform among the people.

This determination is seen throughout the account of his work, even as the book concludes. In the last chapter we see Nehemiah's zeal for the purity of God's people and God's house. We have the picture of a man who was determined to see God honored and obeyed, determined to do God's will for God's pleasure.

What we have seen in Nehemiah 6 is a man who did not allow any of the strategies of the enemy to get him off course. My father on many occasions quoted my grandfather: "Determination, not desire, controls our destiny." Simple and fickle desires are not enough to see us through to the end in doing the will of God. We can easily be knocked off course or find ourselves giving up.

Our Lord Jesus Himself could have called for the chariot to take Him home to heaven after needing to explain His priorities to His own parents when found in the temple courts. He could have ascended back to His heavenly home after the first signs of opposition. He could have given up when His disciples struggled to understand Him or to exhibit the faith they needed. He could have said, "Enough," when He faced the insults, schemes, and challenges of His opponents, who owed their very existence to His creative agency. He could have ascended on high right after the Upper Room discourse, having now prepared His disciples for their role in the future. He could have said, "It is over," in the garden of Gethsemane. He could have said, "Enough is enough," avoiding His sufferings at the hands of false witnesses and the scourging He received. But He went all the way to the cross. He allowed the nails to be driven into His flesh. He allowed His opponents to see His humiliation and defeat from their perspective.

That's because our Lord was committed to the will of the Father. Ultimately it was not His own personal desires; it was only the will of the Father that mattered.

So Jesus finished it. He did it all. He was faithful to the will of God. He was determined to do what God called Him to do. He would not be denied. He was *determined* to do the Father's will. He, of course, is our ultimate example.

A MAN OF DISCERNMENT

In each of the strategies he developed, Nehemiah discerned what was really happening and then acted accordingly. This kind of wisdom or discernment:

- understands the enemy and his schemes
- understands self and personal weakness
- understands the Lord and His strength

Jesus said, "Be wise as serpents and harmless as doves" (Matt. 10:16). The apostle Paul instructed the Colossians to "walk in wisdom toward those who are outside, redeeming the time" (Col. 4:5). Jesus Himself demonstrated such discernment when He faced the evil one in the temptations recorded in the Gospels. In each case He used the written Word of God to counter the schemes of the enemy and to overcome direct opposition to the will of God.

What a need there is for God-given and practical discernment! We should not be naïve about the plots of the enemy, nor of the need for total dependence upon the Lord. A major concern in Paul's epistle to the Colossians, for example, was his desire to heighten his readers' discernment in the midst of deceptive teachings that were threatening their walk with Christ. (See Col. 2:4, 8, 16, 18, 20–23.) We need discernment based on the Word of God and knowledge of the will of God.

A MAN OF DEPENDENCE

We have already noted two of Nehemiah's prayers revealing two different areas of dependence. First of all, He prayed for God's strength at the point of weakness (6:9). Second, he placed his enemies in God's hands and relied upon God's judgment (v. 14).

Where strength is needed, we must look to the Lord. When we have opposition to deal with, we need to present this situation to the Lord, totally handing it over to Him. How easy it is to take matters into our own weak hands—matters that must be given over to and left with God alone. Nehemiah was a man of action, but he knew how to place matters in God's hands as well.

Such verses as 1:11; 2:8 (which speaks of God's "good hand"); 2:18, 20; 4:20, and later verses indicate that Nehemiah consistently looked to the Lord for the accomplishing of His will. He had a sense of being a part of God's plan, and he sought the hand of the Lord throughout his life. Sure, there were special times of prayer, but these times were based on a consistent dependence upon the Lord.

Likewise, of course, we too must depend on the Lord. Christian perseverance is not a "grit your teeth and do things in your own strength" kind of perseverance. We must live in total dependence upon the Lord.

I love the prayer and doxology written at the end of the epistle to the Hebrews, the epistle that expounds what persevering faith really means: "Now may the God of peace who brought up our Lord Jesus from the dead, that great Shepherd of the sheep, through the blood of the everlasting covenant, make you complete in every good work to do His will, working in you what is well pleasing in His sight, through Jesus Christ, to whom be glory forever and ever. Amen" (Heb. 13:20–21).

We must *seek* the work of God in us in order to *see* the work and will of God done through us. This is the essence of the prayer. The same God who powerfully raised our great Shepherd from the dead is the One who in accordance with His own covenant is able to "make [us] complete in every good work to do His will" (v. 21). How? By working in our lives for His own pleasure. We must depend upon the Lord, and such prayers as Hebrews 13:20–21 are good examples of the way we can pray.

It is especially during crises, of course, that you can tell whether or not you are depending on the Lord. In Nehemiah 6 we see a man facing crisis and pressure. At these times Nehemiah directed his attention and his words to the Lord twice, revealing his prayerful dependence upon Him. What a picture we have here of a man totally dedicated to the Lord. This dedication is seen in Nehemiah's determination, discernment, and dependence. Such qualities are needed when doing the will of God in a fallen world.

God-honoring Victories Experienced by Doing God's Will

> And it happened, when all our enemies heard of it, and all the nations around us saw these things, that they were very disheartened in their own eyes; for they perceived that this work was done by our God. (Neh. 6:16)

Troubles were to continue. A great deal of opposition was still to be faced. Nehemiah could not relax as if the struggle was completely over. But the specific task of completing the wall was accomplished in fifty-two days. And there was real significance to the completion of this task. What was accomplished through this God-ordained, God-led, God-accomplished project?

GOD'S PEOPLE WERE BLESSED

The role of the city walls was to protect the people, enabling them to go about their lives with a sense of peace. I don't want to assign principle in a wrong manner, but certainly a common result of doing God's will is the blessing and strengthening of God's people. This project was an important one in the rebuilding and establishing of the people of God. The initial report had told Nehemiah that the people—the survivors—were "in great distress" (1:3). This project was to help the people in that condition as well as take away the reproach of an unprotected broken-down city. What Nehemiah did certainly blessed, helped, and ministered to the people of God.

Blessing and helping God's people must be on our hearts as leaders. Doing God's work in His way will ultimately strengthen God's people.

GOD'S ENEMIES WERE THWARTED

The enemies heard and saw what had been done, and they had to admit that God had brought this about. They had not been able to stop the project. Jesus Himself came to destroy the work of the devil—and the devil himself (Heb. 2:14–18). We must recognize that there are those who desire to see the work of God halted and the name of God disappear. Nothing is worse for God's enemies than to see God do the improbable or the impossible. This task, as simple as we may picture it, was quite an undertaking. We should not have modern construction sites in our minds. And when you add to the equation the attempts to stop the work on the walls, you can see why the enemies would have been "very disheartened in their own eyes" (Neh. 6:16).

We need to rejoice when the evil one is thwarted and the work of God is accomplished. This needs to be a regular, ongoing part of our worship and praise. The only caution is that we need to make sure we are rejoicing in what God has done, not in our own personal advancement or agenda.

God's Power Was Recognized

God is glorified when the help of God is obvious. God was recognized even by His enemies—"For they perceived that this work was done by our God" (v. 16). The celebration on the part of the people of God is recorded later in Nehemiah 12:27–43. Here we read of the dedication and celebration of the completion of the wall with great joy. I am sure God was praised and thanked for seeing them through this project and bringing about this accomplishment.

How exciting it is to be a part of the work of God! This enables us to be about God's will and to know that the resources of God are available to enable us to do what needs to be done.

Many people have been blessed by *Experiencing God*, the study that Dr. Henry Blackaby authored. This account in Nehemiah is a wonderful example of some of the main principles of that study that impacted so many lives for God and for good, such as:

- *Hear God speak.* Nehemiah heard the report concerning Jerusalem.
- *Respond in faith.* Nehemiah prayed and sought an opportunity.
- *Make adjustments in order to do God's will.* The opportunity was given

and Nehemiah acted on it, which meant leaving everything and going to Jerusalem.

God enabled. His will was accomplished. And God was glorified. The doing of God's will ultimately will bring thanksgiving and praise to our God. This was Paul's instruction to the Corinthians as he encouraged them to fulfill their commitment to be a part of the collection project for the poor in Jerusalem:

> For the administration of this service not only supplies the needs of the saints, but also is abounding through many thanksgivings to God, while, through the proof of this ministry, they glorify God for the obedience of your confession to the gospel of Christ, and for your liberal sharing with them and all men, and by their prayer for you, who long for you because of the exceeding grace of God in you. Thanks be to God for His indescribable gift! (2 Cor. 9:12–15)

This was so much more than just a human project. Paul saw this as part of doing God's will in a way that would bring praise and glory to God. And ultimately that is what counts. Bringing glory to God is not a side issue or a last comment after someone gets an award. Bringing glory to God is why we were made, why there is a world, why there is a church, and why there is a purpose and plan of God in this world. It is why we are and it is why we do!

Perseverance Is Needed

As leaders and committed Christians, doing God's will is to be our bread and butter. I sometimes get concerned when I see individuals, churches, ministries, or institutions taking a lot of time to formulate their niche vision or mission statement. Yes, this can be a very fruitful exercise, and it is helpful for everyone within the circle of the organization to know the priorities. But it is most important in this process that the leadership (and all involved) be sure that what is stated is, in fact, God-initiated, God-shaped, God-driven, and God-dependent. The other may be a critical exercise on the part of most organizations going through this self-defining process, but caution is needed to avoid raising our will above the will of God.

Nehemiah was not just doing his own thing because he was good at it. This project was birthed in the revealed condition of the people of God, through passionate prayer and through an amazing answer to prayer. Then the hand of God led and provided all the way, enabling Nehemiah to overcome the strategies of the enemy.

We need to know that God is calling us to do His will, and we need to seek to discern that will. But we also need to expect the attacks of the enemy in the various forms they can take: to distract, destroy, disturb, discourage, deceive, discredit, and more. We should seek the qualities that we have focused on: determination, discernment, and dependence. Then we should work so that God can bring about His results—strengthening His people, thwarting His enemies, and glorifying His name and power.

Is God calling you to a new task, to a new ministry, to a new place of service, to a new mission field? Or are you in the middle of the job? Are you facing opposition and challenge like never before? Are you nearing the end of the mission but the mountains ahead are higher than those you have crossed already?

If you have not done so already, take some time to restate what you consider to be God's will for you in terms of the specific priorities He has given you. God is conforming you to the image of His Son, and you need to be in the center of God's will in your relationships and responsibilities in marriage, family, church, work, government, and so on. But more specifically I am talking about a "calling," a God-given task that you believe to be His will for you right now. Write it out. Commit it to the Lord. Seek His leading. Seek His hand. Seek the qualities needed to give yourself over to this work, whatever it may be. Ask for discernment. Pray often.

Do the work with God's help and for His glory. Finally, recognize that determination and perseverance will be needed. There is a beginning, there is a middle, and there is an end. In order to end well, there has to be perseverance in the work of God.

CHAPTER 9
Praying for Others
COLOSSIANS 1:3-14

I suppose it is possible to be a gifted leader, generally speaking, without a vital prayer life. But in the life of the *Christian* leader, the role of prayer cannot be overestimated. It is not possible to be a faithful Christian, much less a Christian leader, without prayer.

The Old Testament, of course, is full of examples of fervent and effectual prayer, especially voiced by chosen leaders, whether patriarchs, prophets, priests, or kings. Prayer was later part of the curriculum that Jesus taught His disciples (Matt. 6:5–15; Luke 11:1–13). Prayer was displayed in the lives of early church leaders. And prayer has been the vital breath of believers down through the centuries.

Definitions of prayer are like definitions of a sunset; they don't capture the reality, dynamic, and beauty of the subject itself. We know also that there are many different aspects and types of prayer, as the Psalms and other biblical examples reveal. So we would be merely scratching the surface to try to present the various dimensions of prayer.

All true prayer is directed toward God. This may seem obvious, but it is important to stress because the leader lives in the context of people, tasks, problems, pressures, and circumstances. It is possible as a leader to think in a cause-effect framework that leaves God out altogether. The reality of life on the horizontal level can take over, and we can lose the sense of the constant responsibility and joy of being in relationship with the God on whom we must depend for everything—everything!

Prayer for the Christian leader must not merely be a few words voiced before a business meeting or an attempt to "Christianize" human activities and decisions. Prayer should be the regular, if not constant, interchange between the servant of God and the God whom he serves. Dallas Willard has described prayer as "talking to God about what we are doing together."[1] This definition suggests that we are in a meaningful relationship with God and that we discuss mutual concerns together—mentally, internally, as well as outwardly in various forms of expression. True prayer is indeed relational, being based on the covenant relationship that we have with our Heavenly Father, through His Son, by the Holy Spirit. The only qualification I would give to this definition is that "talking" needs to be interpreted very broadly, for prayer involves every form of personal communication, including silence and shouting.

Whatever way you slice it, there is a mystery to prayer that is simply beyond us. We have a risen Lord at "the right hand of God, who ... makes intercession for us" (Rom. 8:34). We have a helper, the Holy Spirit, who "makes intercession for us" at the deepest level and according to "the will of God" (Rom. 8:26–27). Such help is in light of our human weakness and ignorance, both of which are assumed by the apostle Paul in his classic statements from Romans 8. And yet this divine intercession does not replace our own prayer life. We are told to pray. *We must pray.*

We know that prayer changes us. It is part of our cooperation with the work of God in our lives. At the same time, the witness of Scripture declares that our personal prayer is a vital part of how God works in our world. To ask, "What would be accomplished without prayer?" is parallel to asking, "What would be accomplished without God?" since God uses His prescribed means to bring about His purposes. The Scriptures testify to specific things happening in relation to prayer. Prayer is not just a religious exercise for practical deists who really don't need God or recognize His active involvement in the daily affairs of this world. If we would be biblical leaders, we must believe that the personal activity of prayer actually does make a difference. This is one of the primary reasons we must pray as leaders.

Practically speaking, prayer is learned. That does not mean that God prefers the prayers of the learned. The sincere cry of the babe in Christ reaches His open ear. But to use a comparison, married people learn over time various new dynamics and dimensions to communicating with one another that are valuable as the relationship grows. Such is the case in our relationship with the Lord. On the practical level, we learn to pray as we are alone with God and as we pray with others who know how to pray. We learn more about prayer as we read the scriptural truths concerning prayer and put them into practice. We learn how to pray as we allow others who know God to share with us their experience in prayer.

The Leader and Prayer

Leaders battle (or should battle) with conflicting principles and priorities, even after diligently and faithfully studying the Scriptures and consulting wise counselors. The vision may be God-given. The principles may be clear as crystal. The options may be spelled out carefully. But we live in the reality of numerous interrelated decisions with significant consequences. Prayer takes the leader beyond himself, placing him in the presence of the God to whom he is accountable.

More than that, prayer admits and voices dependence upon the only One who is the ultimate source of help and strength. Prayer enables the ministry of the Spirit to operate at a deep level in God's fellowship with those who admit they are ignorant and weak. Prayer helps us make decisions within a conversational relationship with God, the One who loves us and is pledged to work out His will in our lives. There is something about placing matters before the Lord and in His hands that is absolutely fundamental to the life and service of a Christian leader.

I know there have been times when I have failed to do this the way I should, and who knows the consequences of such indiscipline! I praise God for every encouragement to pray by those around me—such as my wife, family, and friends. I am grateful for the regular times of prayer with others on the team over the years. I am thankful for those who have chosen to pray with me on important matters. I rejoice in the knowledge that many people I don't even know by name have interceded for me over the years. Thinking and speaking God-ward must be part of the lifestyle of the leader who wants to function in a Christian manner.

Paul's Thankfulness for the Colossian Church

We could study great prayers of leaders like Moses, David, Solomon, Nehemiah, Jeremiah, Daniel, not to mention examples from the New Testament including our Lord Himself. But I want to direct our attention to the apostle Paul again, listening in on one of his prayers. My goal here is not simply to study prayer as such but to reveal how a leader expresses leadership concerns in prayer. I believe this example will challenge us to pray about important matters in our work or ministry. Even more than that, I hope this example will challenge us to pray for the people we hope to influence or serve.

We return to Paul's letter to the Colossians. The apostle Paul is in chains. He is writing to a church he did not plant himself yet one that he cared about deeply. He had received information about the state of this Phrygian church and the challenges it was facing. Epaphras, a prayer warrior himself (Col. 1:7; 4:12–13), seems to be the immediate human link between the church and Paul, and Paul's letter responds to the news he has received.

After Paul's salutation and greeting, he moves directly into thanksgiving (vv. 3–8). This is a pattern in Paul's letters, but it doesn't diminish the importance of these words of thankfulness. An important part of prayer is thanksgiving. How often do we, even as leaders, focus on what we want God to do and bypass what God has already done? Thankfulness to God is not only appropriate; it is an important part of the leader's worship and perspective.

Simply speaking, Paul is thankful for the Colossians' genuine reception of the truth of the gospel and their genuine experience of its truth. I emphasize the word "truth" because Paul used it twice (vv. 5–6). Truth is clearly a major concern in this letter. Paul certainly did not see the

Colossians' experience as unique, since God was at work in other places, but he was grateful that their experience was real. The gospel had come to them (v. 6). They had "heard and knew the grace of God in truth; as [they] also learned from Epaphras" (vv. 6–7). We must remember Paul's missionary heart, which should be ours as well. It mattered to Paul that the truth of the gospel was proclaimed and that it was heard. We likewise should rejoice and praise God for every evidence of authentic ministry taking place, including the proclamation of the truth of the gospel in the power of the Holy Spirit.

Many years ago I heard the testimony of a godly church leader from Nigeria at a local church function in Memphis, Tennessee. He shared sincere words of thanks for the missionaries who had brought the gospel to his homeland. This was not a small matter to him. We who have grown up in the context of established church life need to recognize afresh the importance of the truth of the gospel reaching people. (This brother in Christ from Nigeria is now the overseer emeritus of a denomination that is seeking to send their own missionaries to share the truth of the gospel, and they have churches in America!)

But these Colossians had a deeper experience than just *receiving* the truth of the gospel. Paul's words reveal that they had a genuine *experience* of the grace of God. They came to know this grace "in truth." No matter what the needs of any individual or church may be, if truth has been received and if there is a genuine experience of the true grace of God, there are reasons for thanksgiving and rejoicing.

Just as in the days of Paul, there are many false and inadequate "gospels" around us. There are cultural gospels that enable us to fit into our communities well. There are self-help messages that encourage people to fulfill their own desires and dreams through various personal attitudes, strategies, techniques, and disciplines. There are mystical gospels, pluralistic gospels, "good works" gospels, and numerous religions and philosophies. So when the true gospel concerning the sovereign Christ and His redemptive work on the cross is proclaimed and received (Col. 1:14–23), there is cause for celebration indeed.

But Paul is specific about what this genuine experience of the gospel looks like. It is seen in the kind of genuine growth exhibited in the lives of the Colossians—their pure faith in the gospel, their love for "all the saints" (v. 4), and their hope of a heavenly inheritance. As we have said, a leader needs to be grateful for the genuine work of God in people's lives. Such thanksgiving should cut through the sham of inauthentic or lifeless activity, no matter how impressive, and praise God for the level of true progress and growth. It is not just a matter of choosing to see the glass half full rather than half empty. We must express thanks for God's gracious working, for without Him nothing of eternal value is taking place.

We must remember that Paul had a clear purpose and definite priorities in ministry. His concern was for the true grace of God being at work in people's lives. Furthermore, he ministered the Word of God so that people would be mature in Christ (vv. 24–29). This, of course, is the purpose of this letter.

By way of contrast, this purpose and the sense of priorities on Paul's part may explain why he withheld thanksgiving as he launched into his strong words in the letter to the Galatians. At stake was the "truth of the gospel" (Col. 1:5). At stake was whether or not they were going to be faithful to the truth he declared during his ministry there. Even in 1 Corinthians, Paul was able to express his thankfulness to God for the giftedness of the Corinthians, which he saw as a real evidence of grace despite the serious problems they were experiencing. Paul could thank God for what really mattered (faith, love, and hope), even when other problems existed.

In verse 7, Paul mentioned Epaphras and commended him for his work and ministry. Epaphras most certainly had shared with Paul what was taking place in Colosse, and Paul commended his faithfulness both to Paul and to his own church. Here we see the horizontal-relational framework for this prayer. Paul had learned about the situation in Colosse from Epaphras, and he used the opportunity not only to commend Epaphras but also to affirm the relationship between himself and the church. Even though Paul had not planted this church, he had a meaningful relationship with the church. Paul knew what was going on, which in and of itself is an important aspect of the ministry of prayer.

Paul also mentioned, sensitively, that Epaphras had communicated to Paul the "love in the Spirit" that the Colossians had (v. 8). One cannot overestimate the importance of affirming real relationship and loving fellowship in the Spirit when it comes to the ministry of prayer. If relationships are strained for whatever reason, this must be put right before meaningful prayer can take place. All of these things combined to give Paul a profound thankfulness for what God was doing in the Colossian church. His prayer for them began with gratitude.

Paul's Intercession for the Colossian Church

If you think for a moment about the prayers we offer on behalf of others, you might find Paul's starting place in Colossians 1:9 unusual. But knowing Paul's heart for his converts as well as his specific concerns in this letter, his starting place makes perfect sense.

Mature Christian Thinking

Paul asked first that God would enable mature Christian thinking on the part of the Colossian believers—"That you may be filled with the knowledge of His will in all wisdom and spiritual understanding" (v. 9). Paul addressed the problem of false teaching and philosophies directly with this prayer. He was not so much praying against what he would address later in the letter (2:4, 8, 16, 18, 20), as he was praying for what he saw as the solution to the problem. Paul was concerned about ideas, philosophies, and practices that were "not according to Christ" (2:8) and were threatening the faithfulness of the Colossians. That's why he prayed specifically for a divine "filling" that leads to the type of thinking that results in right living, faithfulness, and Christian "fullness." For Paul, the antidote to wrong thinking was not to *stop* thinking but rather to possess the right knowledge about the right subject, which would lead to mature Christian thinking. Paul wanted these believers to know that Christ was supreme and sovereign, and that they were complete in Him. One aspect of this completeness was that these believers had access to all the knowledge they needed in Christ. They did not need to be influenced by false teachers or other philosophies, which might lessen their understanding of and devotion to Christ.

For us today, we need to recognize that ultimately knowledge is not found in a new book, a new seminar, a new approach, or a new program except as they are means used by God to communicate His truth. To have a Christian mind, we need a filling with Christ's truth. This is a matter of commitment (Col. 3:2; Rom. 12:2), a matter of ministry—a matter for prayer.

We are living today in an information age, but the information is usually not about God or His will. What a need there is to understand more fully who God is and what His will and purpose are in this world! We need to pray for and seek a greater understanding of God's will for His people. Certain specific aspects of God's will are revealed in the Scriptures for us. And when not, God's priorities and ways are consistently evident enough throughout the Scriptures that with the aid of the Holy Spirit, we can seek to discern and do God's will in the practical aspects of our lives. Such knowledge leads to a worthy walk, a life pleasing to God.

Paul qualified this filling of knowledge about God's will with the words "in all wisdom and spiritual understanding" (Col. 1:9). While divine illumination is certainly fundamental for such full knowledge, Paul would see such knowledge coming primarily through the faithful proclamation, teaching, and admonishing of the truth in Christ (vv. 24–29).

Paul revealed his personal concern for the Colossians along these lines starting in 2:1. His conviction was that such knowledge was to be found in Christ Himself, gained through the means that Christ had ordained for His church (vv. 1–23). It was the responsibility of the church to focus on Christ and to learn from Him through the ministry of the church (3:1-17). Believers were to walk in the truth they had learned, indeed in Christ Himself, and they were to watch out for false wisdom that would cheat them, deceive them, and put them in bondage to legalism. I would see Paul's instruction in this letter to be one of the means that God was using to impart true knowledge "in all wisdom and spiritual understanding" (1:9). And we are the beneficiaries today, as were the Colossian believers in the first century.

MOTIVATED CHRISTIAN LIVING

These believers were to be filled with knowledge for a particular reason: "That [they would] walk worthy of the Lord, fully pleasing Him" (v. 10). He wanted them to have the right motivation. Seeking to live in keeping with the Lord's desire and pleasure did not contradict (in Paul's mind) a life based on the grace of God. Paul would not have entertained the thought of earning God's grace for one moment. At the same time, salvation by grace does not mean that God's purpose, will, or pleasure are not realities of utmost importance for the Christian. God has a real purpose for His people, as well as real pleasures and desires. The believer should passionately seek to live for the Lord's glory and pleasure, recognizing that outside of the grace of God such an endeavor is meaningless and fruitless. It is only as one is "in Christ" that such a pursuit is enabled on God's terms. This matter of honoring the Lord and pleasing Him are the correct motivation for Christian living rather than secondary motivations, like personal fulfillment or ministerial effectiveness.

The Christian leader should be praying for God's glory and pleasure in all matters of service and ministry. Such a prayer must be offered for our own lives and then for the lives of those whom we serve. This concern should dominate decisions and actions. It should be uppermost in the minds and hearts of those we seek to influence. Paul would say later in the letter, "And whatever you do in word or deed, do all in the name of the Lord Jesus, giving thanks to God the Father through Him" (Col. 3:17). Although the wording is different, Paul is stating here the practical outworking of the right motivation for all Christian activity. If we take Paul's teaching in Colossians seriously, a full understanding of who Christ is, what He has done for us, and who we are in Him should contribute to a passionate concern to walk in such a way as to honor the Lord and please Him in all things.

Our prayer for God's glory and pleasure should be no small matter. It is possible to get tremendous external results in leadership contexts with the wrong motivations. Even though it may be hard to admit, the pressure for certain results on the human level may be more present in the leader's mind than the passion to honor and please the Lord. This can be the case for those we influence and serve as well. Certainly we need to *verbally* give God the glory, but the issue is the true motivation of the heart and mind. It is no small prayer that we truly will be more concerned for God's pleasure and honor than our own. The world, the flesh, and the devil all resist the God-centered life, promoting instead the self-centered life. A life with pure motivations is a lifelong battle and will be a lifelong pursuit. So pray accordingly!

MATCHING CHARACTERISTICS

Paul proceeded in his prayer to spell out several important aspects of this motivated Christian lifestyle that pleases the Lord. As we view these marks or characteristics of Christian living, we will gain a sense of Paul's pastoral concern for these believers.

• *Fruitfulness.* Paul's desire for these Colossian believers was that they first of all be fruitful for God in every good work (v. 10). It is so easy to pray for the physical, relational, and practical concerns of people without remembering to view their daily lives in relation to God. Paul saw all of life as lived before God. He also saw that the believer's life should be characterized by *fruitfulness* for God.

This fruit of good works is one of the clear evidences of true spiritual life and growth. The importance of such good works is lost sometimes in the circumstances of life. But no circumstance can hinder the believer from doing good works. Often the focus in prayer is the changing of circumstances instead of being fruitful for God in the midst of whatever the believer is experiencing. It is certainly appropriate to intercede for specific circumstantial and physical needs, and there are plenty of scriptural examples of such prayers. But even though this prayer may seem "generic," it is so important to pray that God's people will be obedient in terms of good works, which is fruit that is pleasing to God.

This matter of good works also brings to mind Paul's letter to Titus. Within a challenging environment, the testimony of good works was a priority concern of Paul (Titus 1:16; 2:14; 3:1, 8, 14). This same concern is expressed here in Paul's prayer. Fruitfulness, productivity, usefulness, and good works are pleasing to God. They are the evidence of a walk worthy of the Lord, and we should be in prayer about them.

• Knowledge. The next focus for prayer is increase in the knowledge of God (Col. 1:10). The outward fruitfulness that we have already considered is now matched with an inner fruitfulness. Growth in the true knowledge of God is an ongoing need for every believer. Here the concern is not God's will or purpose but growth in the knowledge of God Himself. In one sense you cannot think of anything more profound than the knowledge of God in all of His fullness. And yet it is possible to pray for people without thinking about this as their most basic, profound, and continuous need. The Colossian believers needed to grow their knowledge of God in the context of the ideas and philosophies that surrounded them. Just as they needed an awareness of the falsehoods that were "not according to Christ" (2:8), they needed continuous growth in the knowledge of God. Healthy believers and churches are always increasing or growing in their understanding of God, and this should be at the top of our minds as we pray for them.

One might be led to think that such a prayer is not very practical in light of all the personal and everyday needs people have. If tempted to think along these lines, we may want to answer this question: How many issues or problems would be solved or faced more faithfully and effectively if people had a deep, dynamic, and growing knowledge of the living God? Such true knowledge of God and His ways, especially in Christ, would make a great practical difference in many situations and circumstances. I don't think Paul would be tempted to think along these lines at all. In fact, he would see the believer's growth in the knowledge of God as a prerequisite to authentic and continuous Christian experience and growth.

• *Strength.* Strength to endure is Paul's next focus in prayer for these Colossian believers, "strengthened with all might, according to His glorious power, for all patience and longsuffering with joy" (1:11). Paul's words indicate that there was available to the Colossians a resource of power in God Himself that would be adequate for all the circumstances of life. What a prayer! What a resource! What an encouragement for the Colossians and for us today.

What strikes me most about this prayer thrust is how this strength is to be manifested or utilized. Paul wasn't praying here for miraculous interventions, works, or events as such. It is certainly appropriate and necessary at specific times to pray for such mighty demonstrations of divine activity. But here Paul prayed for the ability to endure life's trials with patience and joy. This is one of the greatest testimonies to authentic spiritual life. It takes divine enablement to handle life with patience and joy, especially when circumstances would rob you of both.

I'm sure that specific examples come to mind as you think of people who have evidenced a faith in God that blew you away by their sense of joy, patience, and peace in the midst of harsh storms and relentless winds of suffering. Two people I know come to mind who have handled their bouts with cancer with this kind of grace and trust. And this joyful dependence upon God was not just for a few days or weeks. It has been evident over years of struggle. Such strength does not only point directly to the glorious, gracious provision of God. It is also a great encouragement to other believers. Nothing helps us handle life more faithfully in hard times than to see how another believer is strengthened to endure while exhibiting the peace of patience and the radiance of joy.

Paul would later direct his attention to his own ministry, referring to his dependence on the Lord for the work to which he was called: "To this end I also labor, striving according to His working which works in me mightily" (v. 29). The labor and the striving were realities. But just as real was the mighty working of God. Such power was necessary for ministry and the endurance that Paul needed. Here in Paul's prayer, you sense Paul's desire to see the Colossians experience life with a joyful endurance that can only be explained with reference to a God who enables and empowers.

The personal application for the faithful leader is not hard to see. The leader needs to undergird the "led" with prayer support. Good ideas will take us only so far. Words of encouragement are important, but they are not enough. God's power is needed if we are to do God-shaped things and to live with a God-shaped character. Part of that character involves patience and joy, which are revealed (or revealed missing) in the midst of challenges, labors, trials, suffering, and persecutions that come to the believer. Certainly the leader must find strength in the Lord as well, but here we are concerned about the leader's prayers on behalf of others. We need to point people to their true source of strength and help them see what God is seeking to do in their lives. His power does not always take people *out* of situations. He puts a high priority on character development and on the growth process of believers into Christlikeness. This process takes place through *all* the circumstances of life and is no secondary matter. It is not always about winning the game. It is about how we play and how the game shapes us to be what we ought to be. The leader needs to make sure that his purposes and priorities line up with God's priorities on a day-to-day basis.

• *Thankfulness.* The last characteristic presented in Paul's prayer for the Colossians is actually the first one we considered—thankfulness. This thankfulness is to be directed to the Father, who orchestrates the activities that bring about the salvation Paul went on to describe. The word *salvation* is not used in these verses, but it summarizes the various movements Paul presented for thankful appreciation.

The Colossians had been granted a share in an inheritance that was eternal. Paul seemed to be thinking of the future in 1:12, drawing attention to the inheritance that the Colossians would share with all the saints. Thanksgiving should be offered for what the Father has already done to make that future inheritance a reality. In contrast to "the light," which is the realm of the saints, Paul spoke of what God has done to deliver the Colossians from the "power of darkness" and to transfer them into a new realm, "the kingdom of the Son of His love" (v. 13). The Father had brought these Colossians into His beloved Son's kingdom or realm. The verbs indicate that this had already happened and that it was a radical deliverance.

Paul then expressed the standing of the Colossians not in terms of being in a *kingdom* but being in Christ ("in whom," v. 14). This simple transition may give us insight into the "in Christ" phrase that Paul uses so frequently. These believers were now in the realm of Christ Himself, and therefore *had* experienced, *were* experiencing, or *were going to* experience the realities and benefits of being in Christ's kingdom. Redemption, which seems to relate to "the forgiveness of sins" (v. 14), was something they were presently experiencing due to being in Christ.

It is hard not to be thankful if one is aware of things to be thankful for, and Paul sought to present such things clearly and comprehensively. Obviously the list could be longer, but Paul concisely presented the basic blessings of being in Christ. For all of us in Christ, we can be thankful as we look back at what God has done, as we consider the present experience that is ours in Christ, and as we anticipate the inheritance of the saints. These are all truths that Paul would proclaim and teach, and here they are in the context of prayer and as subjects for thankful reflection. Such thankfulness is a wonderful attribute to see in the character and conduct of God's people.

Prayer and Service

One of the reasons I have chosen this text for study is to see clearly how Paul prayed for the very concerns he was seeking to address. This is more than a literary device in my opinion. I see this as evidence of a prayer life that related directly and purposefully to the apostle's ministry.

Paul prayed about his ministry concerns, prayed about what he did in ministry, and prayed for those he served in ministry. Leaders need to pray meaningfully for those they lead and serve.

It is instructive to note that Paul was not too big to ask for prayer (see Rom. 15:30–33; Eph. 6:19–20; Col. 4:3–4; Philem. 22). Paul valued the prayers of others as part of the process of doing ministry. Paul sensed his dependence on and accountability to the Lord in a direct and personal way. And a primary way that dependence and accountability are revealed is through prayer. Also, the mutual fellowship of prayer is one of the most important means available to us for strengthening relationships at all levels in the body of Christ.

Praying for others is not an option for the faithful Christian leader. Paul exhorted that prayers "be made for all men" (1 Tim. 2:1). The Scriptures are filled with calls for intercessory prayer and examples of the same. I suppose one of the classic statements was made by Samuel who saw it as a sin against the Lord not to pray for the people (1 Sam. 12:23). Jesus not only taught His disciples how to pray (Matt. 6:5–14), but He also prayed for them (John 17:1–26, esp. vv. 9–19). As an exercise, read through our Lord's prayer in John 17. See how closely His prayer is tied to His purpose and priorities in His mission. Here again, we see prayer as a vital part of a God-ward life and ministry. May we serve in the context of prayer, and may we pray in the context of service.

CHAPTER 10
Multiplying Yourself
PHILIPPIANS 2:19–24

Have you ever received a boxed product that had a little slip of paper or sticker inside with a name or number on it? I have. The name or number represented the person responsible for the inspection of the item or product sent. In short, that name or number indicated that the item was indeed "send-able." Someone had inspected the item and authorized that it be sent out.

In Philippians 2:19–24, the apostle Paul was informing the Philippian believers that he intended to send Timothy to them. In the process of informing his readers of this, he commended Timothy as one ready to serve. Paul had inspected Timothy, as it were, and considered him worthy to be sent to Philippi to do what was needed. Timothy was deemed "send-able," so he received Paul's authorization. Why? Because Timothy could be trusted to handle the situation, having been trained and tested by Paul himself. This is how Paul expressed it:

> I trust in the Lord Jesus to send Timothy to you shortly, that I also may be encouraged when I know your state. For I have no one like-minded, who will sincerely care for your state. For all seek their own, not the things which are of Christ Jesus. But you know his proven character, that as a son with his father he served with me in the gospel.
>
> Therefore I hope to send him at once, as soon as I see how it goes with me. But I trust in the Lord that I myself shall also come shortly. (Phil. 2:19–24)

We have already touched on the need for leadership training. Here we will view the goals of such training and consider some of the ways that primary goals can be achieved in leadership training. The result of it should be preparing a given individual to serve.

From Paul's words of commendation and explanation, we are going to learn both the *requirements* and the *assignments* of those who are ready to serve. But to view this subject appropriately, we need to see this marvelous epistle in the context of Paul's ministry and mission. The practical aspects of Paul's mission, as we have seen, can be listed as follows (Acts 14:21–28):[1]

- preaching the gospel (v. 21)
- making disciples (v. 21)
- strengthening disciples (v. 22)
- appointing leaders (v. 23)

The letter to the Philippians needs to be seen within this framework. Paul had preached, disciples had been made, leaders had been appointed, and Paul was now continuing to minister to this church through letters as well as through the representatives he was sending. What Timothy was called to do was not spectacular or earth-shattering. It was, however, part of the great missionary enterprise designed of God, under the lordship of Christ, led by the Spirit, and obedient to the Word. Simple tasks take on great significance when we see them within the broader context of God's mission and glory.

We also need to view these words of Paul in light of the specific thrust of the Philippian correspondence. One of the key concerns of Paul was to challenge the Philippians to have the kind of humility, selflessness, and servant attitude that would promote unity and further ministry. We live in a day of personal convenience and preference, which leads to the lack of a servant mind-set. We are to have the mind of Christ, and this was a major concern of the apostle Paul as he addressed his beloved friends in Philippi.

Finally, note the way this Scripture text begins and ends. Paul says, "I trust in the Lord Jesus to send Timothy to you shortly" (v. 19). Then he says, "But I trust in the Lord that I myself shall also come shortly" (v. 24). This matter of sending Timothy was not some kind of flippant back-up plan. As Dr. Hawthorne states, Paul's "plans and expectations were subject to the Lordship of Jesus Christ."[2]

So we've seen the missionary strategy of Paul, the servant mind-set of Christ, and Paul's conscious submission to the lordship of Christ. Being aware of this contextual framework prepares us to consider the meaning and significance of Paul's words in Philippians 2:19–24.

The Personal Requirements of One Ready to Serve

Paul's commendations give us a picture of someone trustworthy and ready for the task he was asked to do. Timothy was a person characterized by *deep genuine concern*: "For I have no one like-minded, who will sincerely care for your state" (v. 20).

Timothy was special to Paul. He had a kindred spirit. He shared a similar mind-set and heartbeat with the apostle Paul. He was concerned for the Philippians' lives, their well-being, their situation. This is such a simple description of Timothy, and yet what a challenge to me and to you. Someone who can be sent into a given situation needs to have "heartburn," a true concern for others. Paul could entrust Timothy with the task of going to Philippi because he knew Timothy sincerely cared for them. We need to pray that God will give us caring hearts willing to be burdened with the concerns of others.

How much so-called ministry is virtually meaningless because it is not infused with genuine love, genuine passion, and genuine concern. If you read this entire epistle, you will sense the concern that Paul had for these people, being "poured out as a drink offering on the sacrifice and service of [their] faith" (v. 17). Timothy had such a concern.

I remember standing in an airport in the capital city of Honduras.

We had just finished a seminar on expository preaching and were heading to Nicaragua. Our primary translator had been Dr. David Harmes, a man who had spent much of his life as a missionary in Honduras. As my father, mother, and I were about to go to the gate, our little group prayed in a public area of the terminal. I distinctly remember Dr. Harmes praying for "our people." That simple phrase stuck with me. He was not a native Honduran; he had come to Honduras as a missionary. But he was so identified with the people that he very naturally prayed for "our people," not for "those people." He was so deeply concerned for the people that he completely identified with them. His concern was heard and sensed in that prayer and in everything else he did. He had a deep genuine concern demonstrated in nearly forty years of doing almost any and everything a medical missionary can do.

Sadly a person may be in a great place for potential fruitful witness or service, but preoccupation with self or with stuff and not with the state of others will render service ineffective. Timothy had what was necessary to serve because true service must be based upon a deep concern for the state of others. We must pray for the love of God to flood our souls so that we can be usable where we are.

But it is worth noting separately that Timothy also had a deep, genuine concern for the "things" of Christ. There is an overlap between these two concerns, but look at how Paul states this: "For all seek their own, not the things which are of Christ Jesus" (v. 21). Whoever else might have been a potential candidate for going to Philippi did not have the heart, mind-set, or concern of Timothy; they "all" were focused on personal concerns and matters. By way of implicit contrast, Timothy's heart, feelings, and life revolved around "the things" of Jesus Christ.

What challenges me about this phrase is the Christ-centeredness of Timothy. How important this is for a true servant of the Lord. We must be about our Master's business because that is our concern. His concerns are our concerns. Think about it—why would the Lord want to send someone into service who does not have His heart, His concerns? How about you? How about me?

One of my heroes is a missionary named Edith Johnson. Edith has spent more than fifty years in Trinidad. She once told me of the pain she has felt returning to the United States, trying to share her ministry with people here. She did not say this with any bitterness on her part, just the sadness of sensing that her burden was not understood by others. People can easily be caught up in their homes, their things, and not have a real heart for the "things" on the heart of a missionary. Sadly even those who name the name of Christ can sometimes appear to have little interest in His "things." On the other hand, it is beautiful to sense and see the faith of those who passionately love Christ and whose lives revolve around Him and His kingdom. You often see such focus in the lives of those who have very little materially. Jesus means so much to them because they have no rivals to Him in their lives. They really have nothing else. Things, possessions, activities, personal goals, and "stuff" can often pre-occupy us so that our concern for the things of Christ becomes small and really only lip-service. This was not true of Timothy. He had concern for the things of Christ.

He also had *definite proven character*. "But you know his proven character, that as a son with his father he served with me in the gospel" (v. 22). Timothy was trustworthy to Paul because he had already served in such a way as to reveal his character and worth. Let us try to express a few qualities that are revealed or at least implied in what Paul says here.

- Timothy was *loyal*—as a son with his father.
- Timothy was *humble*—he served.
- Timothy was *accountable*—with me.
- Timothy was *experienced*—in the gospel.

Timothy had a track record. He had served with Paul. Implied in these words is the fact that Paul had proven Timothy in experience, and therefore he knew him to be loyal, humble, accountable, and able.

God is looking for such people to use. You may say, "I haven't had that kind of experience!" But are you willing to go and work for the Lord to be shaped and proven? It may be that God is seeking to help you grow right now, where you are, to develop loyalty, humility, accountability, and ability in your life.

For a period of time, a neighbor of ours was in music and youth ministry at a very large church in the area. But the story of how he was called there was surprising. He had been serving as a church janitor in another city—a job he approached very seriously, taking pride in making sure the church was clean. He told me that while he was cleaning a toilet, he received a phone call inviting him to come and minister in music at this large church in Memphis. He said yes. And then the Lord opened up the door to minister at the church for a period of time. The lesson he learned was that he needed to be willing to do *anything* for the Lord.

A servant heart is developed in service. Timothy proved himself by serving with the apostle Paul, which led to Paul being able to send Timothy by himself into situations where someone trustworthy was needed.

These are the simple requirements for someone being ready to go into a position, a place, or a phase of service: *deep genuine concern* and *definite proven character*. Clearly there is a need for specific training when the task calls for specific skills, but if someone is to serve the Lord, they need to have these basic characteristics or requirements.

Leadership Training

We are going to move on to consider what Timothy was supposed to do, but first of all, I want us to think about this matter of leadership training. Timothy was being asked to do something that called for leadership and ministry abilities. Paul had worked with Timothy and mentored him in the crucible of ministry experience. Timothy had proven himself on the job with Paul in various ministry situations in the past.

This speaks to the value of ministry and leadership training that has a strong, practical experience component. People not only *learn* through experience; they are proven and tested through experience. True character traits and skills show themselves as the apprentice works alongside an experienced practitioner. This text from Philippians 2 is certainly not intended as a model for training, but it provides a real-life example for us to consider. And when you add what we learn from Paul's letters to Timothy, you can see how much Paul invested in Timothy in terms of time, instruction, encouragement, exhortation, and much more. Indeed it would be a good exercise right now to go to 1 and 2 Timothy and read through Paul's communications carefully. Paul's love and concern for Timothy can be sensed throughout the letters.[3]

Paul was able to commend Timothy (Phil. 2:19–24) because he knew of his character firsthand and could recommend him with personal knowledge. I have been asked on occasion to write letters of recommendation for people. I am very careful when I do that. I really seek to limit my remarks in the light of my knowledge of the person. It is important for the one receiving the letter to know this so they can understand the basis for comments made. Obviously I try to be as complimentary as I can honestly be, but I can only say what I have experienced to be the case. Paul had no problem in this regard. He had plenty of firsthand experience with Timothy, and that's what personal training calls for and provides.

There are many different types of training needs and models. Try to state what you believe to be the goals of training. You may include some of the following: useful knowledge, practical competence, adequate skills, increased ability. Many others in a taxonomy of learning could be listed. But I want to note something that I think is fundamental to Paul's comments.

There was a uniqueness to Timothy that meant Paul could trust him completely. From the mentor's standpoint, this trust is certainly the primary and practical goal of training—*to know* that you can trust your trainee to be responsible for a given situation. Paul uses a word that captures this uniqueness on the part of Timothy. It is the word translated "like-minded." The word could be translated "like-souled," and it speaks of a shared mind-set and a shared heart about someone or something. I recognize there is a uniqueness to each individual who needs training, so we are not talking about cloning people. But there needs to be a heart-connection, a sharing of core values and understanding that enables the trainer (like Paul) to entrust an important situation into the understudy's hands (like Timothy).

The Philippians were dear to Paul. Their well-being meant much to him. To send someone to them who would not treat them the way Paul wanted them to be treated would have been out of the question. They were like a precious vase that needed to be handled with care. Timothy was the man for the job because he was "like-souled" with the apostle Paul.

True ministry preparation does not involve just the impartation of knowledge. It involves an impartation of values, attitudes, and passions. It involves incarnation and transformation.

The Specific Assignments for One Ready to Serve

"I trust in the Lord Jesus to send Timothy to you shortly, that I also may be encouraged when I know your state. . . . Therefore I hope to send him at once, as soon as I see how it goes with me" (vv. 19, 23). The specific task that Timothy was to accomplish was to check on the Philippians, to see how they were doing, and to inform Paul accordingly. I'm sure ministering to them directly, in person, would be part of that assignment. But if you look closely at the text, you will note that Timothy was not actually to leave right away. There was an immediate need to which he must attend.

Timothy Was to Stay and Serve Where He Was

"I hope to send him at once, as soon as I see how it goes with me" (v. 23). Implicit in Paul's words is the idea that Timothy would come as soon as Paul's situation was clarified. What situation? Paul was facing a very difficult personal crisis. The possibility of death seemed to be right before him, even though he had confidence that he would be delivered

(Phil. 1:19–26). He was praying for deliverance and was hopeful, but his life was on the line. Timothy was there with Paul at a critical time—to do what needed to be done for Paul in the midst of his situation.

Timothy was a true servant. He was ready to go, but he was also willing to stay. God may lead us to stay where we are, but we must be ready to go if necessary. Each believer needs to have this kind of servant attitude—ready to go but willing to stay as needed. And behind that decision is submission to the Lord. In either case you need genuine concern. You must serve on the basis of proven character and serve where you currently are until you're sent somewhere else.

Timothy Was to Go and Serve Where He Was Sent

This is the whole reason behind Paul's words. He was informing the Philippians of Timothy's anticipated arrival. He commended Timothy and authorized his visit, reception, and ministry in Philippi. I cannot imagine Timothy saying something like, "I don't want to go to Philippi! Send someone else! They don't respect me anyway. Come on, Paul, send one of the other guys."

Part of faithfulness is being ready to serve—being ready to stay or go as directed and to do what needs to be done. A few verses before this slice-of-life text in Philippians is the example of our Lord Himself (Phil. 2:5–11). He is the perfect example of one who was willing to go, to let go of heaven itself, and to humble Himself in the most complete way imaginable. He became a humble servant in the form of a man, and He was obedient even to the point of death on a cross. This servant is now the exalted Lord, before whom everyone will bow. Our Lord was faithful as a servant, and we have the same calling. May we be true servants of the Lord.

Personal and practical training is still needed in our day. Yes, people can learn through the use of technology and good educational models. But there is something special about personal training that enables the heart of the leader or teacher to be shared with the learner in real-life situations. And it is within these situations that personal attitudes are challenged and shaped. Practical ministry training enables the leader to see the learner under fire and evaluate his or her character in response to personal challenges and crises. You want to see deep personal concern emerge as ministry takes place. This concern needs to be for people and their situations, as well as straightforward passion for the things that matter to the Lord. There needs to be a Christ-centeredness to servants of Christ! As leaders we not only need to be faithful servants; we need to be faithful in mentoring, teaching, and training others that they might carry on the work of the Lord as servants.

The Christian leader should seek to multiply himself or herself by encouraging, educating, and equipping others to be faithful extensions of their own lives and ministries in the mission of Christ. We are not talking about some sort of narcissistic cloning of "mini-me's." We are talking about the transferring and entrusting of a vision and a passion for Christ-centered ministry, as well as a deep, genuine concern for people.

All Christians are to be involved in discipleship, influencing others to grow in Christ. But those in leadership roles need to be extending that discipleship process, seeking to multiply themselves in terms of service and ministry.

Influencing individuals toward Christ-centered service and passion will take time and energy. Indeed it will take a life lived before and shared with those we seek to equip. The leader may receive criticism for the time he invests in the training and mentoring of others. Evidently this did not change the methods of either Jesus or Paul.

Part Three:
Encouragements to Embrace

CHAPTER 11

Live by Faith

HABAKKUK 2:4; 3:17–19

Certainly one of the critical moments in our Lord's earthly life was the time in Gethsemane before His arrest and all the events of His passion. Despite the presence of the disciples, the Son of God (in a very real sense) was alone with His Father in moments of agony and surrender. The Lord was "troubled and deeply distressed," and He said that His "soul [was] exceedingly sorrowful, even to death" (Mark 14:33, 34). You sense His awareness of the sufferings and separation ahead as He distanced Himself from the others and prayed three times to His Heavenly Father. His surrender was complete. He embraced the will of the Father and was ready to meet His betrayer (v. 42).

There was a uniqueness to these Gethsemane moments that must be recognized due to the uniqueness of our Lord and His sufferings and sacrifice for our sins. Our experience hardly relates. But what I want to draw your attention to is this picture of God's Servant in deep distress, alone with His Father, even in the center of the Father's will. The challenge He faced was not simply the opposition of man but the cost involved in doing the will of the Father in a fallen world. We not only see the Son of God uniquely going to the cross, but we also see our Lord deeply troubled, distressed, and sorrowful as He anticipates what lies ahead in the will of God. And this experience may be shared by many of us who are seeking earnestly to do God's will.

Servants of the Lord, Christian leaders, and people in ministry will all face critical times that will cause "soul distress." This distress will not only take place in light of the specific challenges to be faced; it will also take place as we seek to understand and come to grips with God's will and ways. If you are not already on your knees, there will be times when you are *put* on your knees, if not flattened completely. Furthermore, many of God's servants at such times, if being honest, will wrestle with God for understanding and answers. Here we leave the Gethsemane scene and travel back to the days of Habakkuk the prophet.

I want us to receive encouragement from the Word of God through the remarkable written prophecy of Habakkuk. We are going to consider the inner battle that can accompany the outer realities of ministry. It is one thing to face suffering, opposition, and direct persecution; it is quite another to wrestle with the inner questions and doubts that can accompany such times. Habakkuk was one who sought understanding as he wrestled with the issues of his own day.

Habakkuk ministered at a critical and difficult time in the history of Judah. Israel (in the north) had suffered defeat and disaster already. Judah would soon fall into the hands of the Babylonians (587/586 BC), experiencing destruction, humiliation, and exile. At that time, in the last decades before the exile, wickedness seemed to abound and prevail in Judah. The prophet longed for the righteousness of God and for God's hand of correction and judgment. He wrestled with issues related to the circumstances of his day. He was a prophet with genuine questions and concerns that seemed to flow out of his prophetic calling and zeal.

Through the probing, the prophecy, the prayer, and the praise in this amazing little book of Habakkuk, we can learn much about how we are called to live in difficult times. God's leaders and all His people are called to live through difficult times in the fallen world. Trust and dependence upon God are essential at such times. Indeed, God's word to Habakkuk, in the middle of this book, was and is that "the just shall live by his faith" (2:4). This statement that speaks of a life of faith and faithfulness is quoted three times in the New Testament (Rom. 1:17; Gal. 3:11; Heb. 10:38) and is seen as wholly relevant to understanding the life of faith in the New Testament. So let's learn some lessons concerning the life of faith by gleaning some basic principles from this major minor prophecy! What strikes me as we begin viewing this dynamic prophecy are the honest, personal questions that concern the prophet.

Questions Confronting the Life of Faith

> The burden which the prophet Habakkuk saw. O Lord, how long shall I cry, and You will not hear? Even cry out to You, "Violence!" and You will not save. Why do You show me iniquity, and cause me to see trouble? For plundering and violence are before me; there is strife, and contention arises. Therefore the law is powerless, and justice never goes forth. For the wicked surround the righteous; therefore perverse judgment proceeds. (Hab. 1:1–4)

The prophet begins sharing his deep concerns and personal perplexities with God. It is as if we are listening in on a very honest and personal interaction between the prophet and his God.

> Are You not from everlasting, O Lord my God, my Holy One? We shall not die. O Lord, You have appointed them for judgment; O Rock, You have marked them for correction. You are of purer eyes than to behold evil, and cannot look on wickedness. Why do You look on those who deal treacherously, and hold Your tongue when the wicked devours a person more righteous than he? Why do You make men like fish of the sea, like creeping things that have no ruler over them? They take up all of them with a hook, they catch them in their net, and gather them in their dragnet. Therefore they rejoice and are glad. Therefore they sacrifice to their net, and burn incense to their dragnet; because by them their share is sumptuous and their food plentiful. Shall they therefore empty their net, and continue to slay nations without pity?

> I will stand my watch and set myself on the rampart, and watch to see what He will say to me, and what I will answer when I am corrected. (Hab. 1:12–2:1)

THE QUESTIONS ASKED

The first question is one that has been asked by many believers over the centuries: "How long?" In other words, why does this present situation of wickedness continue, and why doesn't God seem to be doing anything (1:2–4)? This was a question of deep personal concern from someone who longed for righteousness and the vindication of God. And anyone who has a heart for God, truth, and righteousness—anyone who is concerned about the present wicked state of people's lives and the costs it inflicts upon our culture—longs for the intervention of God in direct, powerful ways. "O LORD, revive Your work in the midst of the years" (3:2) was Habakkuk's cry in prayer.

God actually gave Habakkuk a direct answer to his yearning heart and his specific questions. But the answer, as we will soon see, was not the one Habakkuk wanted. God was going to use the Chaldeans (the Babylonians) to discipline His people. So it should not surprise us that Habakkuk continues his cry to the Lord, even in the light of the knowledge of God's plan to use the Babylonians.

Habakkuk's second phase of questioning centers around the question, "Why?" Why is God going to use the Chaldeans to judge His people, using those who are more wicked to punish people who are more righteous (1:12–14)? Habakkuk reveals his genuine concern for the holiness and righteousness of God in this line of questioning. He is not looking for personal gain or comfort. He is honestly wondering at the ways of God in the light of his knowledge of God's character.

Who of God's servants, if they are honest, has not asked "How long?" or "Why?" in the face of circumstances that beckon for the righteous intervention of God? Indeed if one is not vexed by the prevalence of evil in our day and doesn't have a passionate desire for the victory and vindication of righteousness, then there may be a bigger problem. God's servant in such a case may be out of touch with God completely. The prophet's questions do not come from a heart that is cold toward God; rather the prophet is jealous for the Lord's name and His holiness.

THE QUESTIONER ASSESSED

As we have noted, Habakkuk was not a cynic nor an unbelieving critic. Rather he is addressing God directly with these questions, which is instructive in and of itself. He was not simply dumping his doubts on others, nor was he just mulling over mysteries in personal despair. I would characterize Habakkuk's manner as being sincere and submissive. He wanted to hear from God, and he was willing to be corrected. He was seeking to hear from the Lord rather than just posing questions defiantly or in rebellion against the will of God.

When we ask fundamental questions in the light of God's seeming inactivity or revealed activity, we need to examine our own hearts. What is the motivation behind the questions we are asking as we face issues and circumstances that are beyond us? Are we really seeking God's Word, and are we ready to hear and receive what God says? Are we willing to respond obediently if He directs us to do something in light of the circumstances that concern us?

The first chapter of Habakkuk has much more to say than what we have outlined above. It is filled with passion and picturesque language as the conversation between the prophet and the Lord is presented. But one of the lessons I take away from Habakkuk's conversation with God is that we need to direct our heart's desires and struggles to God Himself. We need to voice our honest concerns and questions to the Lord who made us, called us, and redeemed us. God is big enough to hear our cries of confusion and doubt, especially if they are birthed in a desire to see God's glory and righteousness manifested.

Habakkuk clearly received answers from the Lord, and we can learn from the truths God revealed to him. Aspects of God's answers were specific to Habakkuk's time, but the principles represented in these answers are timeless.

The Answers Given for the Life of Faith

The specific answers Habakkuk received are based on truths that are fundamental to the life of faith.

TRUTHS ABOUT GOD

God is a listening God. The fact that the Lord heard Habakkuk is one of the greatest truths to learn from this passage of Scripture. How God answered the prophet specifically is important, but the fact that He heard and answered at all needs to be stressed. It is very frustrating to share your deepest concerns and problems with someone who is not listening! What a thought, that the great God of the universe would bend an ear to hear our cry, our complaints, our doubts, and our concerns.

God is an active God. "I will work a work in your days," the Lord said (1:5). Habakkuk was burdened by the apparent unrestrained advance of wickedness in his day. One can easily draw the conclusion during such times that God is far away, not involved in the affairs of men in any direct way. God declared and revealed to Habakkuk that He was about to work in a specific, historical way. Habakkuk had God's word that He would work to address the situation that concerned Habakkuk. Even if we do not see God at work, God is actively engaged to bring about His purposes in this world. The questioning believer can affirm that God is active and responsive to the cries of His people.

God is a sovereign God. God chose to use the Chaldeans to serve His purpose. This indicates the Lord's sovereignty over the nations, to be sure, but also His divine prerogative to use the means He chooses to accomplish His will. Therefore when it comes to the cry of our hearts, we don't always see what we want to see and we don't always get what we want to get. Yes, God is in control and He is at work, but because He is sovereign, the specific manifestation of His will and activity may be different than we expected or even wanted. This may not be comforting at times, but it needs to be viewed in the light of the next truth.

God is a righteous God. Explicit in this section of the prophecy is the fact that God would deal with the wickedness of the Chaldeans in due season. It is implicit that this "cup of the LORD's right hand" (2:16) would be revealed according to His righteous judgment. God will sovereignly and righteously judge wickedness, and the glorious future vision is of the knowledge of God's glory spreading throughout the earth (v. 14), and all the earth being silent before the Lord in His holy temple (v. 20).

Habakkuk had a passion for righteousness, and his questions and concerns were directly related to this passion. So for Habakkuk, the knowledge that God was active, sovereign, and righteous was not theological gibberish! He desperately wanted God to reveal Himself, to deal with wickedness, and to fulfill His righteous purposes. God revealed truths to Habakkuk related to these concerns. And the fact that God responded to the prophet is a glorious reminder to us of the personal relationship we have and can enjoy with the Lord, even in the midst of crises and soul distress.

We all need to know these truths. People in ministry, leadership, and Christian service *especially* need to know that God is listening, He is at work, He is in control, and He will do the right things. We need to serve with a confidence in God that is not dependent upon the specific circumstances confronting us. We need to live and serve by faith, a faith in God that leads to faithfulness in life and service. How reassuring to know that God is not beaten by the wickedness we see in our world, nor has He ultimately abandoned His people to themselves. Whatever situations concern us in ministry, God is bigger and better. He still hears the cry of His people. He actively and sovereignly works for His righteous purposes and glory.

TRUTHS ABOUT OURSELVES

God also communicated with Habakkuk important truths about what *he* needed to do. A fresh awareness of God and knowledge of God were very important, but what was Habakkuk to do? How was he to respond to the circumstances he was facing?

However one interprets the writing of the vision and the running with the vision (2:2), it is clear that the prophet needed to wait patiently for the "appointed time" for the fulfillment of God's vision and plan. And in needing to wait for it, the prophet really needed to wait on God. Thus the prophet was not going to see immediately what he wanted to see happen. God would be true to His word, but waiting would be necessary for its fulfillment to be seen.

When you are dealing with critical circumstances and issues that cause questions and doubts, one of the hardest things to do is to wait on God and what He is going to do (in His time) to bring about His ultimate purpose. But *we must wait on God* (2:3). We must wait on God's Word, His plan, and His vision, trusting in the promise and the faithfulness of God. This phrase is used so often, but doing it is a real life challenge. That is why everything we know about God is important because otherwise we would not be able to hold onto God in the midst of the wait. And this means that *we must live by faith* (2:4). The basic meaning is that the righteous person—God's person—must "live" a life of faithfulness, a faithfulness that springs from trust or faith in the living God. The New Testament develops this to show that true righteousness is through faith in God. It is not based on confidence in the flesh.

Notice the contrast here between the "proud" and the "just." The proud follow their own path; the just follow God, relying upon Him. Clearly the Lord wanted to stress this truth to His prophet. While waiting on the fulfillment of God's righteous purpose and plan, those who were "just," including the prophet, needed to live faithfully. They needed to live by faith.

This was God's desire for His prophetic leader and His people at a terribly difficult time. Rather than giving in to discouragement and despair that could lead them to disobedience and unfaithfulness, the call was for faithfulness to the Lord and His will. And this same call remains for us today—the call for the same type of surrender modeled by our Lord in Gethsemane, who trusted in the Father and His will even though the cross had to precede resurrection.

The Expressions of the Life of Faith

Habakkuk's prayer (3:1–15) and climactic words of resolve and praise (vv. 17–19) express in a very real sense the spiritual posture of the prophet. It is instructive that the prophet was in communication with and about His God. The relationship was real and passionate. It must be noted that personal communication and interaction with God does not always bring peace (v. 16). Indeed what is heard or understood concerning God's will may cause one to "tremble." Such was the experience of the prophet. Yet his relationship with the Lord was one that caused Habakkuk to reach out to Him in two distinct ways.

PASSIONATE PRAYER

It doesn't take long to sense the passion of the prophet in prayer— "O Lord . . . O Lord" are his beginning words (3:2). The prophet is passionately appealing for God's mercy in the midst of wrath. He desires God's work—salvation in the midst of judgment. The prophet's prayer reveals a respect for God's sovereignty, glory, and power—His everlasting ways, His wrath, and His salvation. In short, the prophet uses language and imagery birthed in the past activity of God in wrath and salvation (the Exodus) as He calls for God's mercy and work in his own day.

Truths about God permeate this prayer. God's activities in the past and His attributes revealed through these activities become the basis for appealing for God's work in the future. Passion, theology, and history blend together as the prophet cries out to God, feeling the awesomeness of what God is planning to do. The prophet reveals his own weakness and fear, as well as his desire to "rest in the day of trouble" (3:16). Such rest would only be possible if the prophet would live by faith and wait on God to fulfill His righteous plan. An indication that the prophet resolved to trust the Lord is found in the closing words of the book.

PROPHETIC PRAISE

I call the following passage "prophetic praise" because not only is it in a prophetic book, but it demonstrates a faith that looks beyond the immediate circumstances and situations of life and grabs hold of the God of salvation.

> Though the fig tree may not blossom, nor fruit be on the vines; though the labor of the olive may fail, and the fields yield no food; though the flock may be cut off from the fold, and there be no herd in the stalls—yet I will rejoice in the LORD, I will joy in the God of my salvation. The LORD God is my strength; He will make my feet like deer's feet, and He will make me walk on my high hills. To the Chief Musician. With my stringed instruments. (Hab. 3:17–19)

Notice first of all, the *resolve* of prophetic praise (vv. 17–18). Despite the description of total fruitlessness, barrenness, and loss, these words ring out powerfully: "Yet I will rejoice" (v. 18). The prophet is making a choice, a decision, a resolve to rejoice in the Lord in the face of blessings withheld and total disaster and loss. The *focus* of prophetic praise is God Himself (vv. 18–19). "The Lord . . . the God of my salvation" (v. 18) is the prophet's joy and cause of rejoicing. The prophet sees beyond the means of God (the Babylonians) and the resulting consequences (judgment and destruction) to God Himself and His ultimate purpose of salvation. Thus the confidence revealed in these words of rejoicing is in God Himself (v. 19). The prophet finds strength in the Lord, a strength that will enable and elevate him despite the circumstances of life. Here we read the words of faith and hope that are called for earlier in the prophecy (2:2–4).

What an amazing end to this incredible book and the issues it presents. One is reminded of the end of Jude, when confidence in God's keeping power is expressed doxologically after the battle for the faith is clearly presented. Here, after revealing the awesome plan and judgment of God that is soon approaching, the prophet cries for mercy and then affirms a faith that has found its resting place in God alone, "the God of my salvation" (v. 18). The prophet has chosen to trust the Lord and find strength in Him.

One could probably express the bottom line truths of this prophecy in just a few words. But one of the reasons for walking through this book is to sense the reality of the struggle, as well as the resolves that come out of that struggle. A leader will deal with difficult and painful issues. I've been there! But these issues are not only external and objective; they can be very internal and subjective. The leader has to wrestle with matters of conscience, matters of truth, matters of understanding, matters that involve coming to grips with the will of God. The Lord may call the leader, the minister, or any of God's servants to walk through something that is extremely costly and painful. The external aspects of the trial may be devastating, but the internal aspects can bring a person to the place of serious questions, doubt, and confusion.

Walking with Habakkuk reveals that there is a place for voicing our questions and concerns to God. The fact that God hears the sincere and submissive cry of His servant at such times is our hope in the midst of distress. There is a place for lament, as we see the world around us and long for the work of God, and it should be directed to God Himself. At the same time, we need to be reminded of fundamental truths about God when we face difficult times and hear afresh His call to live a life of faith and obedience, often waiting for the outworking of His will and plan. Habakkuk provides an example of the type of passionate prayer and prophetic praise that flow out of a heart that has resolved to trust God and find strength in Him. Outward expressions of faith and hope in God are very important at such times. They are choices we make even when we are emotionally spent or crushed. One is not called to be disingenuous but to be both passionate and prophetic in the basic sense of those words.

There are moments of complete "aloneness" in life. God is still present, but no human presence will comfort and no human help will do. As new covenant believers, we can rejoice in the presence of the Holy Spirit and the access we have to the heavenly Father through His Son. But such access and presence do not negate the reality of soul distress that can invade one's inner life at any time. Any or all of the following may be needed at such a time, keeping in mind the other truths of Scripture that can encourage and direct as well:

- Cry out in honest lament.
- Seek to hear from the Lord.
- Believe what you know about God from His Word.
- Wait on the Lord and live faithfully.
- Do what He says.
- Pray passionately.
- Rejoice prophetically.

CHAPTER 12

Do Not Lose Heart

2 CORINTHIANS 4:1–18

Over the last twenty years or so, I have met many people in ministry who are discouraged. On numerous occasions people have come to one of our seminars or training events really needing to be encouraged and strengthened to persevere through hard times. I remember specifically one couple sharing their pain. The wife shared verbally, while the husband just shook with emotion, speechless. The pain in ministry is real and it goes deep. And when you add the day-to-day pressures and problems of leadership, you have a recipe for discouragement, unless the leader or minister can really get a grip.

A classic passage of Scripture for such times is 2 Corinthians 4. I certainly have not been immune to discouragement myself, and that is a personal reason why these words of Paul have been of special help to me. In this amazing section of Scripture, Paul uses the phrase "we do not lose heart" twice (4:1, 16). How did Paul come to this personal conclusion and the resulting lifestyle? It is worth pursuing an answer to this question, for Paul seemed to have a lifestyle of not losing heart. He could praise God, who always led him in triumph in Christ (2:14) as he ministered. In many of his other letters, you sense his victorious spirit and attitude, even in the midst of incredibly difficult circumstances.

At times Paul encourages his converts and churches not to lose heart, not to become weary, but to do "good" (Gal. 6:9; 2 Thess. 3:13). One of his chief concerns, as in his letter to the Ephesians, was to encourage believers not to lose heart at his tribulations (Eph. 3:13). But here in 2 Corinthians he says, "We do not lose heart." He is speaking personally about his own life and ministry. He is not directly encouraging others; he is speaking about his own heart and his own convictions that enabled him to press on victoriously.

It may be that to be faithful in hard times, we need to learn from the apostle's self-disclosure here. It might just be that his reasons for encouragement may help us when we find ourselves "losing heart."

To "not lose heart" is to not become weary to the point of giving up or giving in. "To lose heart" means to despair or to tire so that we stop what we're doing in the Lord's service. Many have stopped or have left the ministry, at least temporarily. Have you stopped doing some things that you know God wants you to do? Have you given up or given in to the pressures and battles you face? Or are you determined by the grace and power of God to press on victoriously for His glory?

This amazing fourth chapter of 2 Corinthians comes in the midst of a letter filled with teaching on ministry, presented by Paul with personal emotion and careful argumentation. He demonstrated that he was not some detached "super apostle" floating above the cares and issues he addressed. No, Paul suffered much in the ministry, and he viewed these sufferings and infirmities as an important aspect of his God-given role.

We are going to focus on three reasons why Paul did not lose heart. But before we look at the first, let's get a sense of Paul's circumstances to see why he *could* have lost heart. He could have sung, "Nobody Knows the Trouble I've Seen."

Right here in 2 Corinthians 4, he speaks of being "hard-pressed on every side," "perplexed," "persecuted," "struck down," "always delivered to death for Jesus' sake." He begins this letter speaking of his afflictions, tribulations, and sufferings in Christ (2 Cor. 1:1–11). Later in his epistle, he lists the various experiences, crises, and sufferings he had to endure (11:23–33; 12:10). For Paul, suffering or the threat of persecution was a way of life.

But there was more involved in Paul's pain than direct opposition from a hostile world. Paul had to deal with the criticisms, questions, and challenges he faced from others in ministry and from his own converts.

In 2 Corinthians, Paul was seeking to explain and defend his own ministry, countering some of the objections and charges against him. What kind of charges? How could people possibly challenge or criticize the apostle Paul?

Well, just to give you a sample of the type of criticisms Paul faced, let me summarize a number from this very epistle:

1) He was thought of as walking according to the flesh (2 Cor. 10:2).
2) He was considered "weak" in person and having contemptible speech (10:10). People didn't think his appearance or presence were much to shout about, and they didn't consider him a good speaker. (That could be discouraging for someone whose primary tasks include preaching, teaching, and leading!)
3) His sphere of authority seemed to be questioned (10:12–17); indeed some thought him to be an inferior apostle (11:5).
4) At times he was·misunderstood and was challenged concerning his practices, such as not being a burden on the Corinthians financially (12:14–21).
5) At a point of argumentation concerning his own ministry, he said, "I ought to have been commended by you" (12:11). Here Paul had to defend himself to his own converts and to the church he planted when they should have been commending him. Such lack of appreciation can drain you of spiritual energy very quickly if you're not careful!
6) He even referred to the Corinthians seeking a "proof of Christ speaking" in him (13:3). It was as if some at Corinth were saying, "Paul, we know that you started this work in Corinth, but are you really a spiritual man? Are you an authoritative apostle?"

Paul had real reasons to be discouraged, to despair, and even to give up and give in. He certainly had reasons to give up on the Corinthians and to let discouragement hinder ministry to these immature people. But no! Paul did not lose heart. He pressed on faithfully and victoriously.

Leaders frequently face hard times. People in ministry often face difficulties. At a seminar in England, I remember hearing a well-known American pastor sharing some of the incredible challenges he had faced in his ministry. As he spoke of various hardships and painful situations, I wondered whether what he was saying was going to connect with his audience. After the seminar, one of the pastors in the audience shared with me that he had experienced the same type of trials and difficulties himself. Such experiences can crush the spirit and cause the leader to question everything. In short, the leader can "lose heart" as we have said. So, what helped keep Paul on track?

It boiled down to the real values that dominated his thinking and living. It had to do with Paul's deep convictions that were the basis for all that he did.

Paul Valued the Gospel Ministry

In the midst of all the turmoil and trouble, Paul was overwhelmed with the surpassing greatness of the ministry he had received and the gospel he preached.

> Therefore, since we have this ministry, as we have received mercy, we do not lose heart. But we have renounced the hidden things of shame, not walking in craftiness nor handling the word of God deceitfully, but by manifestation of the truth commending ourselves to every man's conscience in the sight of God. But even if our gospel is veiled, it is veiled to those who are perishing, whose minds the god of this age has blinded, who do not believe, lest the light of the gospel of the glory of Christ, who is the image of God, should shine on them. For we do not preach ourselves, but Christ Jesus the Lord, and ourselves your bondservants for Jesus' sake. For it is the God who commanded light to shine out of darkness, who has shone in our hearts to give the light of the knowledge of the glory of God

in the face of Jesus Christ. But we have this treasure in earthen vessels, that the excellence of the power may be of God and not of us. (2 Cor. 4:1–7)

For Paul, the gospel and the gospel ministry were so intimately intertwined that we can view them together. Paul had received Christ, had received the gospel, and had received the ministry. Not only that, he *treasured* Christ, *treasured* the gospel, and *treasured* the ministry.

But let's walk through these verses to gain a better understanding of Paul's commitment to the ministry he had received and the gospel he preached.

A MINISTRY RECEIVED WITH MERCY

This ministry was the ministry of the new covenant (2 Cor. 3:6). It was a ministry of the Spirit, the Spirit who gives life (vv. 6, 8). It was a ministry of righteousness and of surpassing glory (vv. 9–11). And due to the ministry and the work of the Holy Spirit, it was a ministry that brought liberty and transformation and glory (vv. 17–18).

Paul was absolutely overwhelmed by and committed to the ministry he had received from the Lord, this ministry of the gospel. It was a ministry that surpassed that of Moses, the great leader and prophet of God. Why? Because this ministry did not bring condemnation; it brought righteousness, life, the Spirit, liberty, and greater glory. Paul treasured what he had received and consequently what he was called to do. Paul treasured this gospel ministry too much to give up.

Paul said that along with this ministry, he had received mercy (4:1), and this enabled him not to lose heart. "Mercy" is a loaded word that will take us all of eternity to understand and enjoy. One scholar and writer speaks of mercy as "that quality in God by which he faithfully keeps his promises and maintains his covenant relationship with his chosen people despite their unworthiness and unfaithfulness."[1] But for Paul, mercy was not just a distant attribute of God; it was something he had experienced from the merciful hand of God Himself. It was due to God's mercy that Paul had been saved on the Damascus Road. It was due to God's mercy that he had been given a privilege and responsibility to proclaim the unsearchable riches of Christ (4:6). Mercy had been received and had undergirded Paul. It came as part of the equipment for ministry. The knowledge and experience of God's mercy enabled Paul not to lose heart as he served this gospel ministry.

A MINISTRY SERVED WITH INTEGRITY

It was because of Paul's overwhelming appreciation for the gospel and the ministry he had been given that he resolved to serve with absolute integrity rather than lose heart and give in. Paul's gospel was a gospel of truth and light. Therefore he would have nothing to do with hidden and veiled things. He made it clear that his ministry had not and would not be conducted in wrong or deceitful ways (v. 2).

This integrity involved specific renunciation. Paul chose not to live or to do certain things. Paul renounced:

- shameful things
- craftiness, trickery
- deceitful handling of the message

In short, Paul would not do anything to shame, distort, or corrupt the truth, thereby tricking and deceiving the people to whom he ministered the Word. Such practices would be completely contrary to the nature of the ministry he had received.

But this integrity involved an open demonstration (v. 2). Paul's ministry was one of opening up, revealing the truth in an honest way so that people could see his integrity in life and message. Someone might challenge Paul here by pointing out that many did not see the truth Paul was declaring. One could question why people did not respond to the truth if it was so clear. They may suggest that the truth was "veiled." Paul goes on to say, "But even if our gospel is veiled, it is veiled to those who are perishing, whose minds the god of this age has blinded, who do not believe, lest the light of the gospel of the glory of Christ, who is the image of God, should shine on them" (vv. 3–4).

The message is truth; it is light. It is not dark or distorted, nor was Paul's method of preaching and ministry. No, the veil over people's eyes is due to the "god of this age" (v. 4). Paul did not need to manipulate truth or people. Yes, some rejected the message or didn't see the truth, but that was and is because of another reason altogether. There are spiritual realities at work, and people are blinded to the light. But Paul would not change his methods or his message despite those who were blinded, those "who do not believe" (v. 4).

A GOSPEL PREACHED WITH SINCERITY

Paul was absolutely sincere in *what* he preached and *why* he preached. His role was one of being a bondservant for Jesus' sake and for those whom he served. Notice he says, "your bondservants" (v. 5). Paul was not taking upon himself the form of an authoritative apostle. He served the Corinthians as a bondservant. He did not preach himself; he *presented* himself as a servant.

Here we see his humble manner in preaching. He exalted "Christ Jesus the Lord" (v. 5), the subject of his preaching. Christ was his message. Paul describes this message in an incredible way. The same God who said, "Let there be light" (Gen. 1:3), had shone the light into Paul's heart. Paul had seen the glory of God in the face of Jesus Christ.

This is one of the great statements that ties together the gospel, Paul's Damascus Road experience, and his resulting ministry. His message was all about light—the light of Christ Jesus the Lord. It was all about truth. The knowledge of God's glory was revealed in Jesus Christ. What a message! What a gospel! What a ministry! What a treasure! Paul did not lose heart because of the overwhelming and inestimable value he placed upon the gospel and the ministry he had received.

Is it not true that what you value becomes especially evident in crisis times? When the house is on fire, the arriving owner will dive into the house to save what is most precious, leaving other things of lesser value behind. And if something or someone of great value is still inside the house, every effort will be made to retrieve it or him or her! The greater something or someone is valued, the more one is willing to do or put up with to gain or serve what is valued. Paul was willing to deal with the trials he was about to list because he valued the glorious gospel of Christ and the ministry of that gospel. Indeed Paul could speak of this gospel (and possibly the ministry as well) as a "treasure" (2 Cor. 4:7). This was Paul's estimate of what he had received—it was a treasure!

Difficult times and crises do cause us to re-evaluate and assess what is important. Such value assessments guide in the decisions that are made during these times. Paul was committed to what he was called to do. He valued highly the ministry he served and the gospel he preached. He was willing to face the hardships in the ministry because of the value he placed on the ministry itself.

Paul Believed in God's Power

Paul proceeded to reveal another reason behind his refusal to lose heart in the midst of his sufferings. The next few verses declare some of the most paradoxical concepts concerning ministry, but they are critical concepts if one is to be encouraged in the midst of seeming disaster or defeat.

> We have this treasure in earthen vessels, that the excellence of the power may be of God and not of us. We are hard-pressed on every side, yet not crushed; we are perplexed, but not in despair; persecuted, but not forsaken; struck down, but not destroyed—always carrying about in the body the dying of the Lord Jesus, that the life of Jesus also may be manifested in our body. For we who live are always delivered to death for Jesus' sake, that the life of Jesus also may be manifested in our mortal flesh. So then death is working in us, but life in you. And since we have the same spirit of faith, according to what is written,

"I believed and therefore I spoke," we also believe and therefore speak, knowing that He who raised up the Lord Jesus will also raise us up with Jesus, and will present us with you. For all things are for your sakes, that grace, having spread through the many, may cause thanksgiving to abound to the glory of God. (2 Cor. 4:7–15)

Paul speaks of the surpassing quality or the outstanding excellence of a power associated with this ministry and treasure. In the face of all the challenges and persecution, Paul had a definite conviction concerning the power of God being at work as he faithfully ministered. Yes, Paul was utterly convinced of the value of what he was doing (vv. 1–7), but he was also convinced that God was at work accomplishing His purpose by means of his excellent power, despite appearances to the contrary.

Some amazing statements are made in this section of Paul's teaching. And at the heart of it is his clear statement of faith. He believed in God's power manifested in weakness. This was not just a passing notion or casual approach to life and ministry. This was a deep conviction. Within these thoughts of Paul are some of the most relevant truths for those experiencing challenge, hardship, suffering, or persecution.

The Purposeful Demonstration of God's Power

Paul speaks of this treasure of the gospel ministry being carried in earthen vessels, pottery, baked clay. Paul was speaking of himself (and those who ministered with him) as the vessel that held the treasure. The clay pots were inexpensive and breakable. They really only served to hold the treasure. But this was true by design. This contrast between the treasure and the clay pot is a purposeful one. God has so designed things that the glory goes to Him. Just as all attention is on the treasure and not the earthen vessel, so God manifests His power in the midst of human weakness so that power is clearly seen to be of God and not of us.

God has designed the demonstration of His power in ministry so that He gets the glory and others are blessed. Paul ends this section by pointing to the fact that ultimately "all things are for your sakes [the Corinthians], that grace, having spread through the many, may cause thanksgiving to abound *to the glory of God*" (v. 15, emphasis mine). That's the way God planned and designed it. At the same time, He designed it so that others are blessed, "for all things are for your sakes" (v. 15). Paul says in verse 12, "So then death is working in us, but life in *you*" (emphasis mine). If our concern is truly the glory of God and the blessing of others, we are willing to put up with trouble and tribulation, knowing that God is still at work in the lives of others for His glory. It is when we are more concerned about ourselves than about others or God's glory that we lose heart.

THE PARADOXICAL DEMONSTRATION OF GOD'S POWER

Paul faced hardships every day, but they did not beat him. Why? Because of the life of Jesus within him. Even though he had a death sentence upon him, even though he was literally a marked man, even though he carried about in his body "the dying of the Lord Jesus" (v. 10), life was being manifested.

How was that life manifested? First of all, it was manifested in the grace that enabled him not to be crushed, not to despair, to be preserved in the midst of the persecutions he faced. God was at work sustaining and delivering. This is how it works—the life of Jesus is manifested even in the midst of weaknesses and sufferings. This is what Paul was emphasizing. He was literally experiencing the crucified life. He was taking up his cross daily, experiencing all the sufferings and hardships of someone totally committed to Christ Jesus the Lord. But in the midst of this committed crucified lifestyle, he was experiencing the life of Jesus. His emphasis was not on just his own experience but also on the results in the lives of others: "So then death is working in us, but life in you" (v. 12). Paul could point to the life that had been communicated to the Corinthians. Through such a ministry, true life had been experienced on the part of the Corinthians. This is how God's power is often manifested. In the midst of suffering and even apparent defeat, God is at work. So the life of

Jesus is manifested both in sustaining grace and in life-giving blessing communicated to others.

A dynamic church leader from Nepal visited us recently here in Memphis, Tennessee. He shared with us parts of his own story—enough to reveal that he has faced real persecution for his faith. He is not alone, for other believers have faced hardship and suffering for their faith in Christ. At the same time, over the past forty years or so, the church of Jesus Christ has grown exponentially in Nepal. God has been working, and life has been manifested in a harsh and hostile environment.

The apostle Paul would not have been surprised by this testimony. He knew the ways of God and the paradoxical display of God's power in the midst of hardship and suffering. Our brother from Nepal expressed concern for our land here in the United States and told us of a special prayer group that prays for America. So not only are they experiencing spiritual life and growth in Nepal, but who knows the impact of their ministry of prayer on our behalf?

THE PREEMINENT DEMONSTRATION OF GOD'S POWER

We have already noted that Paul was confident that God was at work even in the midst of his hardships. He was being sustained. Life was being ministered. Nothing could ultimately stop what God was seeking to do through the gospel and through His servant. And this was all designed to bring greater glory to God! Paul was convinced of the ultimate victory of this power because of something he knew and believed (vv. 13–14)—the resurrection of the Lord Jesus, as well as the confidence he had in his own resurrection and that of the Corinthians. Whatever victory we may experience in daily life is experienced chronologically between the preeminent demonstration of God's power in raising our Lord from the dead, and the great expectation of power when *we* are raised in Christ. Every victory now points to the ultimate victory that again brings glory only to God because only God raises the dead.

So why do we not lose heart? Because God's power is at work. There is such a thing as victory in the midst of suffering. We are "victors in the midst of strife."[2] Christians cannot be defeated ultimately because God's power is still at work in the midst of weakness and suffering. You could not defeat Paul! In the midst of the persecutions, God's power was still at work. If literal death were to be his experience, resurrection would follow. The preeminent display of God's power was in the resurrection of Paul's Lord, and that always was the solid rock to prove the victory that would ultimately come.

Paul Established Eternal Priorities

With such unshakable values and convictions to sustain and maintain, Paul did not lose heart. But let's go further as we consider another aspect of Paul's encouragement in and for ministry—his focus on eternal priorities.

> Therefore we do not lose heart. Even though our outward man is perishing, yet the inward man is being renewed day by day. For our light affliction, which is but for a moment, is working for us a far more exceeding and eternal weight of glory, while we do not look at the things which are seen, but at the things which are not seen. For the things which are seen are temporary, but the things which are not seen are eternal. (2 Cor. 4:16–18)

Paul repeats the phrase "therefore, we do not lose heart" (v. 16) at this point in his presentation. But, he does more than repeat what he has already said. He gives us insight into what really was important to him and how he assessed his present situation.

As we have noted, what you consider to be of utmost importance reveals itself one way or another in times of crisis. How you view things, how you assess matters, how you set priorities will determine how you view anything. For Paul, what counted were the unseen, eternal realities, not the seen, temporal stuff of this world.

THE INNER MAN OVER THE OUTER MAN

Paul honestly admitted that the outer man is perishing. But he took strength in the fact that a daily process of renewal was taking place in the "inward man" (v. 16). This speaks of the new creation in Christ, the redeemed person who is being renewed and transformed from glory to glory by the Spirit of God. God is at work renewing us spiritually, inwardly, and eternally (Eph. 3:14–19; Rom. 12:2). This process is not hindered by the process of perishing that is taking place.

Think of how much attention is given in our culture to maintaining, fixing, or beautifying the outside and prolonging the inevitable. I'm not talking about basic concerns for health and the wonderful medical advances that have been made in so many areas. But just look at the concerns of talk shows, new products, and so much conversation. It's so often on the outer, the perishing, and the stuff that will not last. Paul's priority concern was on the *inner* man—the eternal work that God was doing in Him.

Paul instructed the Ephesians to focus on this renewal process (Eph. 4:20–24). He told the Colossians to seek and set their minds on things above (Col. 3:1–4). His "yet" (2 Cor. 4:16) reminds me of another "yet" we have already seen that speaks of priority and spiritual discernment:

> Though the fig tree may not blossom, nor fruit be on the vines; though the labor of the olive may fail, and the fields yield no food; though the flock may be cut off from the fold, and there be no herd in the stalls—yet I will rejoice in the LORD, I will joy in the God of my salvation. The LORD God is my strength; He will make my feet like deer's feet, and He will make me walk on my high hills. (Hab. 3:17–19)

THE ETERNAL OVER THE TEMPORAL

Paul's expectation concerning the future gave him perspective for the present. How else could he refer to all he was going through as "light affliction, which is but for a moment" (2 Cor. 4:17)? Paul had such a sense of the eternal, his preoccupation was on the greater glory being "accumulated" due to service and suffering in time and space.

You notice that Paul saw himself as a winner on two counts. First of all, he could say that there is really no comparison between the temporal and the eternal. "It will be worth it all when we see Jesus," he could say. But furthermore, the very sufferings were resulting in "a far more exceeding and eternal weight of glory" (v. 17). The implication is that the more trouble here, the greater the reward there. That's unconquerable optimism for you! He would not lose heart. In the overall divine economy, if you suffer now, you receive glory later. That was true compensation despite the realities of the sufferings he faced (1 Pet. 1:6–9; 4:12–19).

THE UNSEEN OVER THE SEEN

Paul equated the seen with the temporal, and the unseen with the eternal. So this is a restatement of the truth he had already mentioned. But his use of these different words is significant and has a special ring in our day. Is not our world totally preoccupied with the seen, the visual, and the tangible? Worldviews and value systems are based on the things we can see. It is so easy to get sucked into this way of thinking:

- numbers
- statistics
- appearances
- attractions
- buildings
- possessions
- stuff
- bigness

Paul affirms that the priority needs to be on the unseen. We need to shut our eyes more often, to focus on the invisible, to be totally satisfied with the eternal and the unseen.

Imagine you are sitting in a small, dark room. People enter carrying guns. They ask you to stand up against the wall. You are asked to renounce allegiance to Jesus Christ as Lord. If you do not renounce Christ, the guns will be used. How you answer at that moment will indicate whether or not you value the inner man over the outer man, whether you value the eternal more than the temporal, and whether the unseen world is as real to you as the seen world. Paul established priorities that focused on the inner man, the eternal, and the unseen.

How do we not lose heart? It has to do with our values, our beliefs, and our priorities. Paul had his reasons for not losing heart. What are yours? What are the reasons you would share with someone for continuing to focus on the "things" of the Lord and not to lose heart? What or who encourages you when the challenges increase and the pressure is on? "Therefore, we do not lose heart" (2 Cor. 4:16).

CHAPTER 13

Trust His Sovereignty and Sufficiency

LUKE 22:24-30

One of the popular metaphors for life these days is "the journey." When people speak of being on a journey, the emphasis is often on the experiences and the process they are going through rather than their final destination. The Christian journey certainly includes experience, process, development, and growth. But the final destination is clear and certain. Furthermore, the journey has been granted and appointed to Christians in this world, and the journey is to be completed with the help of the resources available in Christ. Most importantly, the journey is not traveled alone. The Lord is with us by His Spirit, working out His purpose on our journey for His glory.

In concluding this book, I want to affirm the sovereignty and indeed the sufficiency of our Lord for this journey of faithfulness. Our Lord is watching over our journey. He is with us, committed to us, enabling us by His grace to finish the journey.

The apostle Peter experienced this sovereignty and sufficiency of the Lord in a remarkable way on his journey. Ultimately Peter was to have a central role in the life, growth, and ministry of the early church. He was a critical and influential leader, to say the least. But, honestly, it is amazing that Peter ended up having any role at all!

This fisherman was called by our Lord to follow Him, specifically to "catch men" (Luke 5:10; see also Mark 1:16–20). Peter (along with the others) "forsook all and followed Him" (Luke 5:11). He spent time with the Lord. He heard His teachings. He saw His miracles. He went on ministry trips with Him and for Him. Peter was affirmed by the Lord for His great confession according to divine revelation (Matt. 16:17). His future significant role in the building of the church was prophesied (v. 18). And yet, the Scriptures record that Jesus had to rebuke Peter strongly when he attempted to correct our Lord (v. 23). Talk about mountain and valley experiences! Peter seemed to have them all.

Later we see Peter at the beginning of Acts as a leader "in the midst of the disciples" (1:15). It seems that the group of disciples recognized his leadership even when awaiting the "promise." Then, filled and empowered by the Holy Spirit, Peter became the preacher on the Day of Pentecost, explaining prophetically what was taking place and proclaiming Jesus as both Lord and Christ (Acts 2). Peter was involved in various miraculous events, and his boldness was evident as he faced opposition and persecution. He was sent to Samaria along with John when the gospel was embraced there (8:14–25). God used Peter, after giving him direct revelatory instruction, to take the gospel to a Gentile, indeed to *the* Gentiles (Acts 10). This was a critical moment in redemptive history, and Peter was there. He is last seen in Acts participating in the Jerusalem Council, which affirmed "that through the grace of the Lord Jesus Christ we shall be saved" (15:11). Peter certainly was used strategically and dynamically to fulfill the purposes of the Lord in the preaching of the gospel and the building of the church. Tradition tells us much more about the latter years of Peter's life, but the biblical text tells us enough to know that he was mightily used of the Lord.

We need to go back, though, to a time in Peter's journey when there was serious turbulence. The setting is right after the Lord's Supper and before Gethsemane. For some reason there was a discussion about being considered the greatest! Jesus gave His clear teaching on this leadership issue in Luke 22:24–30, asking, "Who is greater, he who sits at the table, or he who serves? . . . Yet I am among you as the One who serves" (v. 27).

Yet right after these words of correction and rebuke, we read that Jesus said, "Simon, Simon! Indeed, Satan has asked for you, that he may sift you as wheat. But I have prayed for you, that your faith should not fail; and when you have returned to Me, strengthen your brethren" (vv. 31–32).

What an amazing series of statements by our Lord! Sadly Peter didn't seem to understand or accept what Jesus said. Rather he boasted about his readiness to suffer and even die for His Lord. I guess you could say that Peter was still on a journey! But I want us to move beyond Peter's unique experience to see a number of critical truths based on these words of Jesus. Embracing these truths will help us be overcomers and complete the journey of faithfulness.

First of all, there is a spiritual battle that is beyond our limited understanding. Jesus informed Peter of a spiritual plot that related to his life! Remember Job? Now we need to remember Peter! The Scriptures give us specific truths concerning the spiritual warfare we face, but I think we would be very arrogant indeed to assert that we understand it all. We must put on the armor (Eph. 6:10–19) and learn to resist the devil (1 Pet. 5:8–9). This "sifting" of the disciples (of Peter especially) seems to have been allowed by God according to His ultimate purpose and glory. But to a limited degree, Satan was going to "have at it" with the disciples. So under the sovereignty of our God, there was a spiritual battle to be fought. And there still is! It is beyond us, but it is under Him. This should make us thankful for the sovereignty and sufficiency of our Lord. This should make us ever aware of our desperate need for His help. The problems and challenges we face daily as we seek to live faithfully for Him cannot simply be reduced to naturalistic or strictly human explanations. There are spiritual realities impacting our lives, and we must depend on a spiritual God who knows it all and is over it all. We should be grateful also for the victory of Christ in which we stand (Col. 2:15), and we need to wear the armor He has provided.

This leads me to the second important truth: Jesus said He prayed for Peter. How important do you think the prayer of Jesus was in this context? I don't believe that Jesus would have mentioned it if it was not vitally significant. Peter may not have grasped the simple yet profound majesty of these words. I can't claim that I understand them myself. But I am thrilled to think of our Lord Jesus, fully aware of Peter's weakness and future failure, speaking of His prayer on Peter's behalf. What a picture of our Lord's commitment to Peter and His expectation that Peter would come through the time of testing to future ministry. Maybe this gives us an insight into the present intercessory ministry of our Lord. He is *for* us (Rom. 8:31–34). He is ministering on our behalf to strengthen us, especially in times of trial. We may not fully appreciate how dependent we are on our Lord! He is now our Great High Priest (Heb. 4:14–16). He is ministering on our behalf. Without His atonement and His ministry on our behalf, we are lost.

Third, so often our faith is the battleground. It is our faith that is tested, tried, and purified. Jesus prayed specifically for Peter's "faith" that it would not fail completely. Our faithfulness is directly tied to our faith. Frequently it is the focus and maturity of our faith that will determine how we handle what comes our way. It is interesting that Peter speaks of the importance of the "genuineness of . . . faith" in his first epistle (1 Pet. 1:7). Such faith is "more precious than gold," and will bring "praise, honor, and glory at the revelation of Jesus Christ." Genuine faith, therefore, is not just important for the journey but is important when we reach the destination as well. The Lord is purposely seeking to work on our faith for His greater glory. This is one of the purposes of trials along the way (4:12–13).

Fourth, sin and failure call for a return to Him. Sin and failure are always to some degree a departure or a moving away from the Lord. Sin is unfaithfulness to the Lord. So there is the need for a return, which speaks of full repentance. This does not necessarily mean it will be a long process, but it does indicate a relational dynamic that must be honored in our walk with the Lord. Grace is glorious and amazing, but it doesn't negate the fact that if we walk away or turn away from the Lord, we need to come back to that place of close fellowship with Him (1 John 1:7–9). What is especially encouraging in Jesus' words is that He *anticipates* this return in Peter's life. Our Lord knows the beginning, the end, and the journey in between. He knew what was going to happen and speaks of "when" Peter was to return, not "if." What mercy, love, and grace are shown by our Savior, knowing of Peter's failure and his need to return, and yet looking ahead to his restoration! The Lord Himself sought this restoration of Peter, as we will see.

Fifth, we see the expectation and call for future ministry. "Strengthen your brethren" (Luke 22:32). The Lord did not give up on Peter, despite his temporary disloyalty. Peter had an important role to play. The Lord anticipated future ministry after the sifting and the returning. What I want us to see here is the fact that our Lord saw beyond the immediate crisis to the future leadership role and service required of Peter. He was to strengthen the brethren. Our Lord has the total journey in view. This does not mean, as we consider our journeys today, that the Lord bypasses necessary discipline or that restoration always means returning to the same place of authority or service. There are plenty of examples of serious discipline in the Scriptures. These are critical issues beyond the scope of my concluding remarks. What I want us to see is the sovereignty and sufficiency of our Lord throughout the journey and His commitment to us as His disciples and servants. Peter would not have had a chance if the Lord was not committed to him and his ministry. We don't stand a chance either, except for the Lord's enablement.

This continuing gracious commitment to Peter was fleshed out at the breakfast meeting by the Sea of Tiberias, recorded in John 21. Our Lord questioned Peter's love, and Peter affirmed his love for the Lord—*with humility*. Maybe the sifting experience had taught him something! Peter certainly sounded different in this encounter with the Lord than he had when blowing off the Lord's remarks in Luke 22, convinced that he would not fail. Now in John 21, the Lord commissioned Peter afresh to "Feed My lambs. . . . Tend My sheep. . . . Feed My sheep" (vv. 15–17). But the challenge was really summed up as Jesus told Peter afresh, "Follow Me" (v. 19). Indeed this charge to Peter was reaffirmed when he expressed concern about another disciple, John. Jesus said, "If I will that he remain till I come, what is that to you? You follow Me" (v. 22).

Despite the twists and turns in his journey, Peter's calling from Christ remained the same: "Follow Me." Such a call is essentially to faithfulness based on love—faithfulness to the end of the journey.

This is our calling as well. We are called to follow Him, our Lord and Savior. We are called to faithfulness in life, loyalty, and service. It is a miracle that anyone makes it! But such is the purpose and work of our sovereign and gracious God.

He is able to take us through the powerful forces of this world that would undo us without His aid. He ministers on our behalf, supplying grace upon grace, as well as the resources necessary to live the life and fight the fight. He prays. He prays. He prays. Hallelujah, He prays!

We are His projects as He purifies our faith. Circumstances are used for His purposes in our lives so that our faith in Him will be genuine and lasting. He calls us back when we fail. Sin must be faced and dealt with, but the goal is more than the restatement of our vows. It is restoration toward fruitfulness.

The Lord wants to use us for His glory. Our part is simply to follow—to follow Him lovingly, to follow Him faithfully, regardless of others. We know that He loves us and is committed to us. This is our confidence as we seek to be faithful to Him. Daily it should be our delight—and our duty—to answer the most important question: "Do you love Me?" If we truly can answer daily, "Yes, Lord, I love You," then the journey of faithfulness will be fruitful for His glory.

"And who is sufficient for these things?" (2 Cor. 2:16).

"Our sufficiency is from God" (3:5).

Lead on!

Endnotes

PREFACE

1. "Great Is Thy Faithfulness," words: Thomas O. Chisholm; music: William Runyan; © 1923, renewed 1951 Hope Publishing Company, Carol Stream, IL 60188. All rights reserved. Used by permission.

INTRODUCTION

1. These comments concerning the numerous facets of the election process in the U.S. were made many months before election day 2008. This does not reflect on any candidate or the outcome of any election, but simply the usual dynamics of any election year.
2. Ted Engstrom, *The Making of a Christian Leader* (Grand Rapids: Zondervan, 1976), 20.
3. J. Robert Clinton, *Leadership Perspectives: How to Study the Bible for Leadership Insights* (Altadena, CA: Barnabas Publishers, 1993), 21.

CHAPTER 1

1. For a careful, technical treatment of this text, see Steve Walton's presentation in *Leadership and Lifestyle: The Portrait of Paul in the Miletus Speech and 1 Thessalonians*, Society for New Testament Studies Monograph Series, 108 (Cambridge University Press, 2000). Dr. Walton views Paul's speech in light of parallels, especially in 1 Thessalonians. Such parallels strengthen the case for Luke's account, giving us an accurate picture of the same Paul who wrote 1 Thessalonians.
2. F. F. Bruce, *The Acts of the Apostles: The Greek Text with Introduction and Commentary* (Chicago/Toronto: InterVarsity, 1952), 377.
3. Ibid., 382.

4. Jon Mohr, "Find Us Faithful." ©1987 Jonathan Mark Music (administered by Gaither Copyright Management) and Birdwing Music (a division of EMI Christian Music Publishing).

CHAPTER 2

1. For a more in-depth study of the gospel of grace, read *The Secret of Soul Winning* by Stephen Olford (B&H Publishing Group, 2007), 43–62. I had the privilege of contributing this chapter.

2. For more information, read "Chapter 1: Renewing the Quest for the Historical Kerygma," in *The Gospel and Its Meaning: A Theology for Evangelism and Church Growth* by Harry L. Poe (Zondervan, 1996), 15–55.

3. Ted S. Rendall, "Ezekiel: Called to be a Watchman for God." Sermon. (The Stephen Olford Center for Biblical Preaching, Memphis, TN), May 16, 2005.

CHAPTER 4

1. Besides various commentaries, a section of an unpublished doctoral thesis dealt with sacrificial language in Romans 15:16. See David Olford, "An Exegetical Study of Major Texts in Romans which Employ Cultic Language in a Non-Literal Way" (Sheffield: University of Sheffield, 1985), 356–430.

CHAPTER 5

1. Walter A. Elwell, ed., *Baker Encyclopedia of the Bible, Volume 2* (Grand Rapids: Baker Book House, 1988), 1,222–23.

CHAPTER 6

1. *MacArthur Study Bible: New King James Version* (study notes), ed. John MacArthur (Word Publishing: Nashville, TN), 1988.

2. A biblical and practical resource for spiritual warfare is Ray Pritchard's *Stealth Attack: Protecting Yourself against Satan's Plan to Destroy Your Life* (Chicago: Moody Publishers, 2007).

Chapter 7

1. There may have been sociopolitical issues and protocol at work in this situation, but Paul does not address this matter on that level. What is dynamic is the fact that he deals with this situation on the basis of love.

2. Richard R. Melick, Jr., *The New American Commentary: An Exegetical and Theological Exposition of Holy Scripture, Volume 32: Philippians, Colossians, Philemon* (Nashville: Broadman Press, 1991), 335.

3. If there were any legal issues at stake, Paul certainly does not refer to them.

4. Frank E. Gaebelein, ed. *The Expositor's Bible Commentary, Volume 11* (Grand Rapids: Zondervan, 1978), 462.

5. Loving relationships need to start in the home. I have not devoted a chapter to marriage and family issues, knowing that there is much available in print on the subject and sensing that the subject was too big for me to tackle. Having said this, the basic principle referred to in this chapter can be applied to family relationships as well, keeping in mind the directives and patterns that the Scriptures give us (Gen. 2:18–3:24; Eph. 5:22–6:4; Col. 3:18–21; 1 Pet. 3:1–7; 1 Cor. 7:1–40; 11:3–16). We must pursue loving and right relationships at all levels, starting with husband-wife, parent-child relationships.

Chapter 8

1. I am grateful for the discussion of Nehemiah 6 in Walter C. Kaiser, Jr.'s, *Toward an Exegetical Theology: Biblical Exegesis for Preaching and Teaching* (Grand Rapids: Baker, 1981), 205–210. My approach to the text has been influenced greatly by his work.

2. Dr. Hershael York, professor of Christian preaching at Southern Seminary, Louisville, Kentucky, was referring to Sir George Mallory, a famous mountain climber, who died on a climbing expedition. His message, "Cut Me Some Slack," was preached at a Biblical Preaching Institute in June 2006 at our center in Memphis.

CHAPTER 9

1. Dallas Willard, *The Divine Conspiracy: Rediscovering Our Hidden Life in God* (San Francisco: HarperCollins Publishers, 1997), 243.

CHAPTER 10

1. Leroy Zumack, a missionary serving in France at the time, drew my attention to this text and its picture of priorities in missionary work and church planting in a message he presented at the Stephen Olford Center for Biblical Preaching a number of years ago.

2. Gerald F. Hawthorne, *Word Biblical Commentary: Volume 43, Philippians* (Waco, TX: Word Books), 109.

3. Paul's mentoring of and instructions for Timothy are used as a guide for preachers today in the book *Anointed Expository Preaching* by Stephen Olford and David Olford (Nashville: Broadman & Holman Publishers, 1998). See chapter 2—"The Preacher and the Word of God," 19–28; chapter 4—"The Preacher and the Man of God," 38–49; chapter 5— "The Preacher and the Work of God," 50–65. My father wrote these specific chapters.

CHAPTER 12

1. Walter A. Elwell, ed., *Baker Encyclopedia of the Bible, Volume 2* (Grand Rapids: Baker Book House, 1988), 1,440.

2. "Joyful, Joyful, We Adore Thee," hymn, Henry J. Van Dyke, 1852–1933.

Bibliography

Armstrong, John H., ed. *Reforming Pastoral Ministry: Challenges for Ministry in Postmodern Times*. Wheaton, IL: Crossway Books, 2001.

Arndt, William F., and F. Wilbur Gingrich. *A Greek-English Lexicon of the New Testament and other Early Christian Literature*. Chicago: The University of Chicago Press, 1963.

Barna, George, ed. *Leaders on Leadership: Wisdom, Advice, and Encouragement on the Art of Leading God's People*. Ventura, CA: Regal Books, 1977.

Boa, Kenneth. *Conformed to His Image*. Grand Rapids: Zondervan, 2001.

Bridges, Charles. *The Christian Ministry with an Inquiry into the Causes of Its Inefficiency*. Edinburgh, Scotland: The Banner of Truth Trust, 1997.

Bruce, Alexander Balmain. *The Training of the Twelve*. Grand Rapids: Zondervan, 1963.

Cedar, Paul, Kent Hughes, and Ben Patterson. *Mastering the Pastoral Role*. Portland, OR: Multnomah Press, 1991.

Clinton, J. Robert. *The Making of a Leader*. Colorado Springs: NavPress Publishing Group, 1988.

Cousins, Don, Leith Anderson, and Arthur DeKruyter. *Mastering Church Management*. Portland, OR: Multnomah, 1992.

Covey, Stephen R. *Principle-Centered Leadership*. New York: Fireside Books, 1992.

Dobson, Edward G., Speed B. Leas, and Marshall Shelley. *Mastering Conflict and Controversy*. Portland, OR: Multnomah, 1992.

Eims, LeRoy. *Be the Leader You Were Meant to Be: What the Bible Says about Leadership*. Wheaton, IL: Victor Books, 1975.

Ellis, David J., and W. Ward Gasque, eds. with an appreciation by F. F. Bruce. *Essays on the Church and Its Ministry in God's Community*. Wheaton, IL: Harold Shaw Publishers, 1979.

Engstrom, Ted W. *The Making of a Christian Leader*. Grand Rapids: Zondervan, 1976.

Finzel, Hans. *The Top Ten Mistakes Leaders Make*. Wheaton, IL: Victor Books, 1994.

Ford, Leighton. *Transforming Leadership: Jesus' Way of Creating Vision, Shaping Values and Empowering Change*. Downers Grove, IL: InterVarsity Press, 1991.

Getz, Gene A. *Elders and Leaders: God's Plan for the Church*. Chicago, IL: Moody Press, 2003. *The Measure of a Man*. Ventura, CA: Regal Books, 1995.

Habecker, Eugene B. *Rediscovering the Soul of Leadership*. Wheaton, IL: Victor Books, 1996.

Hendricks, Howard, and William Hendricks. *As Iron Sharpens Iron*. Chicago, IL: Moody Press, 1995.

Hendrix, Olan. *Management for Christian Leaders*. Grand Rapids: Baker Book House Publishers, 1988.

Hughes, R. Kent. *Disciplines of a Godly Man*. Wheaton, IL: Crossway Books, 1991.

Hughes, R. Kent, and Barbara Kent. *Liberating Ministry from the Success Syndrome*. Wheaton, IL: Tyndale House Publishers, 1987.

Larson, Craig Brian, and David L. Goetz. *Pastoral Grit: The Strength to Stand and to Stay*. Minneapolis: Bethany House Publishers, 1998.

London, H. B., Jr., and Neil B. Wiseman. *Pastors at Risk: Help for Pastors, Hope for the Church*. Wheaton, IL: Victor Books, 1993.

Lutzer, Erwin. *Pastor to Pastor: Tackling the Problems of Ministry*. Grand Rapids: Kregel Publications, 1998.

MacArthur, John, Jr., and The Master's Seminary Faculty. *Rediscovering Pastoral Ministry*. Dallas: Word Publishing, 1995. *Shepherdology: A Master Plan for Church Leadership*. Panorama City, CA: The Master's Fellowship, 1989.

Maxwell, John C. *Partners in Prayer*. Nashville, TN: Thomas Nelson, Inc., 1996. *The 21 Irrefutable Laws of Leadership: Follow Them and People Will Follow You*. Nashville, TN: Thomas Nelson Publishers, 1998.

Merkle, Benjamin L. *40 Questions about Elders and Deacons*. Grand Rapids: Kregel, Inc., 2008.

Myra, Harold, and Marshall Shelley. *The Leadership Secrets of Billy Graham*. Grand Rapids: Zondervan, 2005.

Newton, Phil A. *Elders in Congregational Life: Rediscovering the Biblical Model for Church Leadership.* Grand Rapids: Kregel Publications, 2005.

Olford, Stephen. *Basics for Believers.* Colorado Springs: Victor/Cook Publishing, 2003. *Fresh Lessons from Former Leaders.* Grand Rapids, MI: Baker Publishing Group, 1991. *Not I but Christ.* Wheaton, IL: Crossway Books, 1995. *The Secret of Soul Winning.* Nashville: B&H Publishing Group, 2007. *The Way of Holiness.* Wheaton, IL: Crossway Books, 1998.

Pearcey, Nancy. *Total Truth: Liberating Christianity from Its Cultural Captivity.* Wheaton, IL: Crossway Books, 2005.

Peterson, Robert L., and Alexander Strauch. *Agape Leadership: Lessons in Spiritual Leadership from the Life of R. C. Chapman.* Littleton, CO: Lewis and Roth Publishers, 1991.

Phillips, John. *The Life and Legacy of Stephen Olford.* Memphis, TN: Olford Ministries International, 2006.

Pritchard, Ray. *He's God and We're Not: The Seven Laws of the Spiritual Life.* Nashville: Broadman & Holman Publishers, 2003.

Redpath, Alan. *The Making of a Man of God: Studies in the Life of David.* Westwood, NJ: Fleming H. Revell Company, 1962.

Richard, Ramesh. *Soul Vision: Ensuring Your Life's Future Impact.* Chicago: Moody Publishers, 2004.

Rush, Myron. *Management: A Biblical Approach.* Wheaton, IL: Victor Books, 1986. *The New Leader: A Revolutionary Approach to Effective Leadership.* Wheaton, IL: Victor Books, 1987.

Sanders, J. Oswald. *Spiritual Leadership: Principles of Excellence for Every Believer*. Chicago: Moody Press, 1994.

Saucy, Robert L. *The Church in God's Program*. Chicago: Moody Press, 1972.

Sorrell, Bob. *The Next Step: A Seven-Step Planning Process to Help Fulfill Your God-Given Vision*. Friendswood, TX: Baxter Press, 2001.

Stark, David. *Christ-Based Leadership: Applying the Bible and Today's Best Leadership Models to Become an Effective Leader*. Bloomington, MN: Bethany House Publishers, 2005.

Stevens, R. Paul. *Liberating the Laity: Equipping All the Saints for Ministry*. Downers Grove, IL: InterVarsity Press, 1985.

Stott, John. *A Call to Christian Leadership*. London, England: Marshalls and The London Institute for Contemporary Christianity, 1984.

Stowell, Joseph M. *Shepherding the Church*. Chicago: Moody Publishers, 1997.

Thompson, Robert R. *Organizing for Accountability: How to Avoid Crisis in Your Nonprofit Ministry*. Wheaton, IL: Harold Shaw Publishers, 1991.

Whitney, Donald S. *Spiritual Disciplines for the Christian Life*. Colorado Springs: NavPress, 1991.

Woodbridge, John D. *Great Leaders of the Christian Church*. Chicago: Moody Press, 1989.

Youssef, Michael. *The Leadership Style of Jesus*. Atlanta: Leading the Way with Dr. Michael Youssef, Atlanta, GA, 2000.